Traditional Kentucky Recipes

© Copyright 2016. Laura Sommers.
All rights reserved.
No part of this book may be reproduced in any form or by any electronic or mechanical means without written permission of the author. All text, illustrations and design are the exclusive property of
Laura Sommers

Introduction 1

Kentucky Bourbon Whiskey BBQ Sauce 2

Kentucky Biscuits 3

Kentucky Banana Pudding 4

Kentucky Bacon Milk Gravy for Biscuits........................5

Kentucky Chocolate Bourbon Pecan Pie 6

Kentucky Pecan Pie..7

Kentucky Hot Brown 8

Kentucky Hot Brown dip 9

Kentucky Bourbon Sweet Potatoes 10

Kentucky Home Fries 11

Kentucky Fried Green Tomatoes 12

Kentucky Tomato Soup...13

Kentucky Bourbon Balls 14

Kentucky Blackberry Cobbler 15

Kentucky Apple Butter 16

Kentucky Butter Cake 18

Louisville Rice Salad 20

Kentucky Derby Bourbon Punch 21

Kentucky Bourbon Wieners..22

Traditional Kentucky Burgoo 23

Kentucky Jam Cake..25

Kentucky Fruit Filling	27
Kentucky Henry Bain's Sauce	28
Kentucky Derby Pie	29
Louisville Benedictine Spread	30
Kentucky Modjeska Candy	31
Kentucky Fried Chicken	33
Kentucky Style Scalloped Potatoes	35
Kentucky Chicken with Bourbon Jelly	36
Kentucky Style Carrots	37
Kentucky Style Chicken and Dumplings	38
Kentucky Green Tomato Pickles	39
Kentucky Apple Dumplings	40
Kentucky Beer Cheese	41
Kentucky Baked Beans	42
Kentucky Baked Ham	44
Kentucky Bluegrass Salad	44
Kentucky Bluegrass Fudge Pie	46
Kentucky Black Bottom Pie	47
Kentucky Bourbon Cake	47
Kentucky Bourbon Apple Pie	49
Kentucky Chews	50
Kentucky Breakfast Grits Cakes	51
Kentucky Derby with Bourbon Whipped Cream	53
Kentucky Bourbon Whipped Cream	54

Kentucky Cabbage Casserole 55
Bluegrass Beercheese Melts with Bourbon BBQ Glaze 56
Kentucky Chili 58
Kentucky Coleslaw 59
Kentucky Pimento Cheese Sandwich 60
Bluegrass BBQ Chicken 61
Kentucky Cornbread 62
Kentucky Cream Candy 63
Kentucky Eggnog 63
Kentucky Lace Cakes 64
Old Fashioned Kentucky Nut Cake 65
Kentucky Mint Julep 66
Kentucky Fried Apples 67
Kentucky Derby Cheese Grits 68
Appalachian Fried Dandelions 69
Kentucky Fried Corn 70
Appalachian Slaw 71
Kentucky Fried Steak 71
Kentucky Peach Cobbler 72
Kentucky Plum Cake 73
Kentucky Praline Popcorn 74
Kentucky Egg Scramble 75
Kentucky Spiced Tea 76

Kentucky Style Green Beans	77
Kentucky Shaker Corn Sticks	78
Kentucky Bourbon Burgers	79
Kentucky Derby Salsa	80
Kentucky Derby Chocolate Chip Cookies	81
Kentucky Shaker Lemon Pie	82
Kentucky Shaker Fried Chicken	84
Kentucky Shaker Tomato Pudding	85
Kentucky Shaker Flank Steak	86
Kentucky Shaker Spiced Apple Pudding	87
Kentucky Spoonbread	88
Kentucky Sausage Cheddar Spoonbread	88
Kentucky Style BBQ Pork Chops	90
Kentucky Pulled Pork	91
Kentucky Mock Turtle Soup	92
Kentucky Brownies	93
Kentucky Eggs	94
Kentucky Ham Biscuits	95
Kentucky Frogs' Legs	96
Kentucky Mountain Oysters (Lamb Fries)	97
Appalachian Stack cake	98
Louisville Rolled Oyster	100
Kentucky Fried Catfish	101
Kentucky Baked Catfish	102

Kentucky Barbecued Catfish	103
Kentucky Catfish Stew	104
Kentucky Fried Okra	104
Kentucky Okra and Tomatoes	105
Kentucky Pickled Okra	106
Kentucky Country Chicken Fried Steak	107
Kentucky Corn Pudding	109
Kentucky Whiskey Chicken	110
Kentucky Black Barbecue Sauce and Mutton Dip	111
Kentucky Country Style Quiche	112
Kentucky Hot Brown Pizza	113
Kentucky Chipotle Pork Quesadillas	114
Kentucky Butternut Squash Soup	116
Kentucky Corn Chowder	117
Kentucky Kale and Potato Soup	118
Kentucky Onion Soup	119
Kentucky Bourbon Beef Stew	120
Kentucky Mock Mint Julep	121
Kentucky Country Ham Balls	122
Kentucky Bourbon Banana Bread	123
Kentucky Bourbon Pecan Sticky Buns	124
About the Author	127
Other Books by Laura Sommers	128

Introduction

The Commonwealth of Kentucky is known as the Bluegrass State based on the grass which grows in its fertile pastures and the style of country music that evolved from the region. Along with Bluegrass, Kentucky also intersects the Appalachian Mountains at the East. Many wonderful mountain country dishes come from there.

Kentucky is known for its own unique form of barbecue. Owensboro, Kentucky is home to the International Bar-B-Q Festival, which is an annual barbecue competition.

Some things are similar to the style of traditional Southern dishes, but with their own unique Kentucky flair.

The Kentucky Derby is held on the first Saturday in May every year in Louisville, Kentucky. This is the first and most famous horse race of the Triple Crown which consists of three races run by thoroughbred horses three years of age. The other two races are the Preakness in Maryland and the Belmont in New York. Famous chefs create special recipes just for this very prestigious event.

In Pleasant Hill, Kentucky, the Shakers lived from 1805 to 1910. It is now a tourist destination with many delicious foods and recipes.

Kentucky Bourbon Whiskey BBQ Sauce

Ingredients:

1/2 onion, minced
4 cloves garlic, minced
3/4 cup bourbon whiskey
1/2 tsp. ground black pepper
1/2 tbsp. salt
2 cups ketchup
1/4 cup tomato paste
1/3 cup cider vinegar
2 tbsps. liquid smoke flavoring
1/4 cup Worcestershire sauce
1/2 cup packed brown sugar
1/3 tsp. hot pepper sauce, or to taste

Directions:

1. In a large skillet over medium heat, combine the onion, garlic, and whiskey.
2. Simmer for 10 minutes, or until onion is translucent.
3. Mix in the ground black pepper, salt, ketchup, tomato paste, vinegar, liquid smoke, Worcestershire sauce, brown sugar, and hot pepper sauce.
4. Bring to a boil. Reduce heat to medium-low, and simmer for 20 minutes.
5. Run sauce through a strainer if you prefer a smooth sauce.
6. Serve while listening to some Kentucky Bluegrass music and enjoy!

Kentucky Biscuits

Ingredients:

2 cups all-purpose flour
2 1/2 tsps. baking powder
1/2 tsp. baking soda
1 dash salt
1 tbsp. white sugar
1/2 cup butter
3/4 cup buttermilk

Directions:

1. Preheat oven to 400 degrees F (200 degrees C).
2. In a bowl, mix the flour, baking powder, baking soda, salt, and sugar.
3. Cut in 1/2 cup butter until the mixture resembles coarse crumbs.
4. Mix in the buttermilk.
5. Turn out onto a lightly floured surface, and knead 2 minutes.
6. Transfer to an ungreased baking sheet, roll into a 6x6 inch square, and cut into 12 even sections. Do not separate.
7. Bake 15 minutes in the preheated oven, until a knife inserted in the center of the square comes out clean. Separate into biscuits, and serve hot.
8. Serve while listening to some Kentucky Bluegrass music and enjoy!

Kentucky Banana Pudding

Ingredients:

1 cup white sugar
1/4 cup cornstarch
1 egg, beaten
1 (12 fluid oz.) can evaporated milk
1 1/2 cups milk
2 tsps. vanilla extract
1 (12 oz.) package vanilla wafers 4 banana, sliced

Directions:

1. In a saucepan over medium heat, combine the sugar, cornstarch, egg, evaporated milk and regular milk.
2. Mix together well and stir until thick. Remove from heat.
3. Add vanilla and mix well.
4. In a large bowl or casserole dish, arrange a layer of cookies.
5. Pour pudding mixture over cookies and top with a layer of sliced bananas.
6. Refrigerate until chilled.
7. Serve while listening to some Kentucky Bluegrass music and enjoy!

Kentucky Bacon Milk Gravy for Biscuits

Ingredients:

1/4 cup bacon drippings
1/4 cup all-purpose flour
1 tsp. salt, or to taste
1 tsp. ground black pepper, or to taste
4 cups milk, divided

Directions:

1. Heat bacon drippings in a skillet over medium heat; whisk flour into drippings until smooth.
2. Reduce heat to low and cook the flour mixture until it turns a caramel brown color, stirring constantly, about 15 minutes.
3. Be careful, the roux burns easily.
4. Stir in salt and black pepper.
5. Whisk 1/2 cup milk into the roux until thoroughly blended.
6. Continue whisking milk into the gravy, 1/2 cup at a time, whisking in each amount of milk completely before adding more.
7. Bring gravy to a simmer and whisk constantly until thick, smooth, and bubbling.
8. Serve while listening to some Kentucky Bluegrass music and enjoy!

Kentucky Chocolate Bourbon Pecan Pie

Ingredients:

1 (9 inch) pie shell 1 cup white sugar
1 cup light corn syrup
1/2 cup butter
4 eggs, beaten
1/4 cup bourbon
1 tsp. vanilla extract
1/4 tsp. salt
6 oz. semisweet chocolate chips
1 cup chopped pecans

Directions:

1. Preheat oven to 325 degrees F (165 degrees C).
2. In a small saucepan combine sugar, corn syrup, and butter or margarine.
3. Cook over medium heat, stirring constantly, until butter or margarine melts and sugar dissolves. Cool slightly.
4. In a large bowl combine eggs, bourbon, vanilla, and salt.
5. Mix well.
6. Slowly pour sugar mixture into egg mixture, whisking constantly.
7. Stir in chocolate chips and pecans.
8. Pour mixture into pie shell.
9. Bake in preheated oven for 50 to 55 minutes, or until set and golden.
10. Serve while listening to some Kentucky Bluegrass music and enjoy!

Kentucky Pecan Pie

Ingredients:

1 cup white corn syrup
1 cup packed brown sugar
1/3 tsp. salt
1/3 cup butter, melted
3 eggs
1 cup chopped pecans
1 recipe pastry for a 9 inch single crust pie

Directions:

1. Combine syrup, sugar, salt, and melted butter or margarine.
2. Slightly beat the eggs, and add to sugar mixture.
3. Beat well, and pour into uncooked pie shell. Sprinkle pecans on top.
4. Bake at 350 degrees F (175 degrees C) for 50 to 60 minutes.
5. Serve while listening to some Kentucky Bluegrass music and enjoy!

Kentucky Hot Brown

The Hot Brown was first served in Louisville's Brown Hotel.

Ingredients:

1/2 cup butter
6 tbsps. all-purpose flour
3 cups milk
1/2 cup freshly grated Parmesan cheese, divided
1 egg, beaten salt and pepper to taste
1 tbsp. butter
2 cups sliced fresh mushrooms
1 tomato, thinly sliced
1 pound thinly sliced cooked turkey
8 slices bread, toasted
8 slices bacon, cooked

Directions:

1. In a large skillet, melt 1/2 cup butter over medium heat.
2. Stir in enough flour to absorb all of the butter.
3. Slowly whisk in the milk, and 6 tbsps. of Parmesan cheese.
4. Stir in the egg to thicken the sauce, but do not allow to boil.
5. Remove from heat, and season with salt and pepper to taste.
6. Heat remaining tbsp. of butter in a small skillet.
7. Saute mushrooms in the butter until soft.
8. Set aside.
9. Preheat your oven's broiler.
10. For each Hot Brown, place two slices of toast onto a heatproof plate or dish.
11. Cover the toast with about 1/4 cup sauteed mushrooms and a couple of tomato slices.
12. Place a liberal amount of turkey onto each Hot Brown, and pour an even more liberal amount of sauce over. Smother that baby.

13. Sprinkle remaining Parmesan cheese over the top.
14. Repeat with remaining ingredients.
15. Place the entire dish under the broiler until the sauce is speckled brown and bubbly.
16. Remove from broiler.
17. Criss-cross two slices of bacon on top.
18. Serve while listening to some Kentucky Bluegrass music and enjoy!

Kentucky Hot Brown dip

Ingredients:

3 oz. cream cheese
1/2 cup sour cream
1/2 cup mayonnaise
1/2 tsp. chicken flavored instant bouillon
1/8 tsp. cayenne pepper
2 tbsps. grated Parmesan
3/4 cup shredded Swiss cheese
1 small roma tomato, seeded and chopped
1/2 cup diced, cooked turkey breast
2 slices bacon, crisp and crumbled
2 tsp. chopped fresh parsley

Directions:

1. In a small mixing bowl, combine cream cheese, sour cream, mayonnaise, bouillon and cayenne pepper.
2. Let stand for 15 minutes. Stir again to ensure that bouillon is dissolved. Spread in bottom of 9-inch glass pie plate.
3. Sprinkle Parmesan cheese over cream cheese mixture.
4. Top with Swiss cheese, tomato, turkey and bacon.
5. Garnish with parsley.
6. Chill until ready to serve. Serve with crisp crackers or chips.
7. Serve while listening to some Kentucky Bluegrass music and enjoy!

Kentucky Bourbon Sweet Potatoes

Ingredients:

1 cup white sugar
1/2 cup butter
1/2 cup bourbon
1/2 tsp. vanilla extract

Directions:

1. Preheat oven to 350 degrees F (175 degrees C).
2. Arrange sweet potatoes in a 9x13 inch baking dish.
3. Combine sugar, butter, bourbon and vanilla extract in a large saucepan and heat to a boil.
4. As soon as the sauce comes to a boil pour it over the sweet potatoes.
5. Bake 30 to 40 minutes or until the sweet potatoes are soft.
6. Serve while listening to some Kentucky Bluegrass music and enjoy!

Kentucky Home Fries

Ingredients:

2 tbsps. bacon drippings
4 large potatoes, peeled and sliced
1/2 Vidalia onion, chopped salt and pepper to taste

Directions:

1. Heat the bacon drippings in a large skillet over medium heat.
2. Add potatoes and onion, and stir to coat.
3. Cook, stirring occasionally, until potatoes are tender and golden brown, about 15 minutes.
4. Season with salt and pepper.
5. Serve while listening to some Kentucky Bluegrass music and enjoy!

Kentucky Fried Green Tomatoes

Ingredients:

1/2 cup bacon grease
1/3 cup all-purpose flour
3/4 cup cornmeal
1/4 tsp. ground black pepper
1 egg 1/4 cup milk
1 green tomato, cut into
1/4 inch slices

Directions:

1. Heat the bacon grease in a large skillet over medium heat.
2. In one small bowl, stir together the flour, cornmeal and pepper. In another small bowl, whisk together the egg and milk using a fork.
3. Dip the tomato slices into the egg and milk, then coat with the dry mixture.
4. Place the breaded tomato slices in the hot bacon grease. Cook until browned on each side, about 3 to 4 minutes per side.
5. Bacon grease burns easily, so adjust your heat if you need to.
6. Serve while listening to some Kentucky Bluegrass music and enjoy!

Kentucky Tomato Soup

Ingredients:

3 tbsps. butter
1 cup chopped onion
1/2 cup chopped carrots
2 stalks celery, chopped
2 cloves garlic, minced
1/4 cup chopped fresh flat-leaf parsley
2 1/2 cups chopped fresh tomatoes
1 (8 oz.) can tomato sauce
3/4 cup strong brewed coffee
1/4 cup water
1 tsp. white sugar
1 tsp. salt
Ground black pepper to taste
1/3 cup heavy cream

Directions:

1. Melt the butter in a stock pot over medium heat.
2. Stir in the onion, carrots, celery, garlic, and parsley; cook and stir until the onion has softened and turned translucent, about 5 minutes.
3. Add the tomatoes, tomato sauce, coffee, water, sugar, salt, and pepper. Bring the soup to a boil and simmer for 20 to 25 minutes.
4. Pour the hot soup into a blender, filling the pitcher no more than halfway full.
5. Hold down the lid of the blender with a folded kitchen towel, and carefully start the blender, using a few quick pulses to get the soup moving before leaving it on to puree.
6. Puree in batches until smooth and pour into a clean pot. Stir in the cream and heat until warm.
7. Do not boil.
8. Serve while listening to some Kentucky Bluegrass music and enjoy!

Kentucky Bourbon Balls

Ingredients:

1 cup chopped nuts
5 tbsps. Kentucky bourbon
1/2 cup butter, softened
1 (16 oz.) package confectioners' sugar
18 oz. semisweet chocolate

Directions:

1. Place the nuts in a sealable jar.
2. Pour the bourbon over the nuts.
3. Seal and allow to soak overnight.
4. Mix the butter and sugar; fold in the soaked nuts.
5. Form into 3/4" balls and refrigerate overnight.
6. Line a tray with waxed paper.
7. Melt the chocolate in the top of a double boiler over just-barely simmering water, stirring frequently and scraping down the sides with a rubber spatula to avoid scorching.
8. Roll the balls in the melted chocolate to coat.
9. Arrange on the prepared tray.
10. Store in refrigerator until serving.
11. Serve while listening to some Kentucky Bluegrass music and enjoy!

Kentucky Blackberry Cobbler

Ingredients:

6 cups fresh blackberries
2 tsps. lemon juice
1 cup white sugar
2 tsps. cornstarch
1/4 cup cold butter, cubed
4 cups all-purpose flour
1/4 cup white sugar
1 tsp. ground cinnamon
1 tbsp. salt
1 tbsp. baking powder
2 tsps. baking soda
1 cup chilled butter, diced
1 1/3 cups buttermilk, plus additional for brushing
1/4 cup white sugar

Directions:

1. Preheat an oven to 375 degrees F (190 degrees C).
2. Butter a 9x13-inch baking dish.
3. Place the blackberries in a mixing bowl, and sprinkle with lemon juice.
4. Toss with 1 cup sugar and cornstarch until evenly coated.
5. Place into the prepared baking dish, and arrange the cubes of butter on top.
6. In a large bowl, whisk the flour, 1/4 cup sugar, cinnamon, salt, baking powder, and baking soda together.
7. Cut in 1 cup of chilled, diced butter using a pastry cutter until the butter is in pieces no larger than a pea.
8. Stir in the buttermilk until a batter has formed. Spoon the batter evenly over the blackberries.
9. Brush the top of the batter with additional buttermilk to moisten, then sprinkle with the remaining 1/4 cup of sugar.

10. Bake in the preheated oven until the the fruit is tender, and the biscuit top is golden, about 25 minutes.
11. Serve while listening to some Kentucky Bluegrass music and enjoy!

Kentucky Apple Butter

Ingredients:

5 pounds McIntosh apples, chopped
1 cup white sugar
1 cup brown sugar
1/4 cup butter
1 tbsp. ground cinnamon
1 tsp. ground ginger
1 tsp. ground nutmeg
3 (1 pint) canning jars with lids and rings, or as needed

Directions:

1. Place apples in a large pot and cover with water; bring to a boil.
2. Reduce heat to low; simmer, stirring occasionally, until apples are softened, 5 to 10 minutes.
3. Preheat oven to 325 degrees F (165 degrees C).
4. Press apples through a food mill to separate seeds, cores, and skin from apple pulp and transfer pulp to a bowl. Stir white sugar, brown sugar, butter, cinnamon, ginger, and nutmeg into apples. Pour apple mixture into a 9x13-inch baking pan.
5. Bake in the preheated oven, stirring and scraping sides every 20 to 30 minutes, until apple butter is red and thickened, 2 to 4 hours.

6. Sterilize the jars and lids in boiling water for at least 5 minutes. Pack apple butter into the hot, sterilized jars, filling the jars to within 1/4 inch of the top. Run a knife or a thin spatula around the insides of the jars after they have been filled to remove any air bubbles. Wipe the rims of the jars with a moist paper towel to remove any food residue. Top with lids, and screw on rings.
7. Place a rack in the bottom of a large stockpot and fill halfway with water.
8. Bring to a boil and lower jars into the boiling water using a holder. Leave a 2-inch space between the jars. Pour in more boiling water if necessary to bring the water level to at least 1 inch above the tops of the jars. Bring the water to a rolling boil, cover the pot, and process for 30 minutes.
9. Remove the jars from the stockpot and place onto a cloth-covered or wood surface, several inches apart, until cool. Once cool, press the top of each lid with a finger, ensuring that the seal is tight (lid does not move up or down at all). Store in a cool, dark area.
10. Serve while listening to some Kentucky Bluegrass music and enjoy!

Kentucky Butter Cake

Ingredients:

3 cups unbleached all-purpose flour
2 cups white sugar
1 tsp. salt
1 tsp. baking powder
1/2 tsp. baking soda 1 cup buttermilk
1 cup butter
2 tsps. vanilla extract
4 eggs
3/4 cup white sugar
1/3 cup butter
3 tbsps. water
2 tsps. vanilla extract

Directions:

1. Preheat oven to 325 degrees F (165 degrees C). Grease and flour a 10 inch Bundt pan.
2. In a large bowl, mix the flour, 2 cups sugar, salt, baking powder and baking soda.
3. Blend in buttermilk, 1 cup of butter, 2 tsps. of vanilla and 4 eggs.
4. Beat for 3 minutes at medium speed. Pour batter into prepared pan.
5. Bake in preheated oven for 60 minutes, or until a wooden toothpick inserted into center of cake comes out clean. Prick holes in the still warm cake. Slowly pour sauce over cake. Let cake cool before removing from pan.

Butter Sauce Directions:

1. In a saucepan combine the remaining 3/4 cups sugar, 1/3 cup butter, 2 tsps. vanilla, and the water.
2. Cook over medium heat, until fully melted and combined, but do not boil.

3. Serve while listening to some Kentucky Bluegrass music and enjoy!

Louisville Rice Salad

Ingredients:

1 cup uncooked white rice
2 cups water
1/2 cup vegetable oil
1/4 cup lemon juice
1/4 cup wine vinegar
1 tsp. white sugar
1 tbsp. chopped fresh chives
1 tbsp. chopped fresh tarragon
1/2 tsp. salt
1/2 cup toasted slivered almonds (optional)
1/2 cup raisins (optional)
1/2 cup mandarin orange segments, drained and coarsely chopped (optional)
1/2 cup finely chopped onion (optional)
1/2 cup finely chopped celery (optional)
1/2 cup finely chopped green bell pepper (optional)
1/2 cup green peas (optional)

Directions:

1. Bring rice and water to a boil in a saucepan over high heat.
2. Reduce heat to medium-low, cover, and simmer until the rice is tender and the liquid has been absorbed, 20 to 25 minutes.
3. Let rice cool for at least 30 minutes, stirring several times as it cools.
4. Transfer to a large salad bowl.
5. Mix vegetable oil, lemon juice, wine vinegar, sugar, chives, tarragon, and salt together in a bowl until the sugar and salt have dissolved.
6. Pour dressing over the cooled rice and stir to combine.
7. Mix your choice of slivered almonds, raisins, mandarin orange segments, onion, celery, bell pepper, and peas into the rice mixture and lightly toss to combine.

8. Cover salad and refrigerate until chilled, at least 1 hour.
9. Serve while listening to some Kentucky Bluegrass music and enjoy!

Kentucky Derby Bourbon Punch

Ingredients:

34 fluid oz. bourbon
1 (12 fluid oz.) can frozen orange juice concentrate, thawed
1 (12 fl. oz.) can frozen lemonade concentrate, thawed
1/4 cup lemon juice
1/4 cup maraschino cherry juice
1 1/2 liters club soda
1 lemon, sliced
1/2 cup maraschino cherries, halved

Directions:

1. Mix bourbon, orange juice concentrate, lemonade concentrate, lemon juice, and maraschino cherry juice together in a pitcher until base is well mixed.
2. Pour the base into a punch bowl.
3. Add club soda, lemon slices, and maraschino cherry halves.
4. Serve while listening to some Kentucky Bluegrass music and enjoy!

Kentucky Bourbon Wieners

Ingredients:

1 (16 oz.) package hot dogs, cut into bite-size pieces
1/2 cup bourbon whiskey
1/2 cup ketchup
1/2 cup brown sugar

Directions:

1. Place hot dogs, bourbon whiskey, ketchup, and brown sugar into a saucepan over medium heat.
2. Heat, stirring often, until the brown sugar has dissolved and sauce is bubbly, 10 to 15 minutes.
3. Serve while listening to some Kentucky Bluegrass music and enjoy!

Traditional Kentucky Burgoo

Ingredients:

3 tbsps. olive oil
1 pound cubed pork shoulder roast
1 pound cubed beef stew meat
4 cups chicken broth
1 1/2 pounds bone-in chicken parts
2 cups diced potatoes
1 cup diced carrots
1 (15 oz.) can stewed tomatoes
1 cup smoky barbeque sauce
1 cup green beans
1 cup diced okra
1 cup corn
3/4 cup diced onion
1 green bell pepper, seeded and diced
1/2 cup diced celery
1/4 cup apple cider vinegar
1 tbsp. Worcestershire sauce
3 cloves garlic, chopped
3 bay leave
1 tsp. salt
1/2 tsp. ground black pepper
1 dash hot pepper sauce, or to taste

Directions:

1. Heat olive oil in an 8-quart pot over medium heat; brown pork and beef cubes in the hot oil, working in batches if necessary.
2. Stir in chicken broth, chicken pieces, potatoes, and carrots.
3. Bring to a boil, reduce heat to low, and simmer stew for 1 hour.

4. Stir in stewed tomatoes, barbeque sauce, green beans, okra, corn, onion, green bell pepper, celery, apple cider vinegar, Worcestershire sauce, garlic, bay leaves, salt, black pepper, and hot pepper sauce.
5. Bring stew back to a boil, reduce heat to low, and simmer 1 more hour.
6. Discard bay leaves before serving stew in bowls.
7. Serve while listening to some Kentucky Bluegrass music and enjoy!

Kentucky Jam Cake

Ingredients:

1 cup butter, softened
2 cups white sugar 5 eggs
1 tsp. baking soda
1 cup buttermilk
3 cups all-purpose flour
1/4 tsp. salt
1/2 tsp. ground cinnamon
1 tsp. ground cloves
1 tsp. ground allspice
1 cup dates, pitted and chopped
1 cup grape jam
1 cup chopped pecans
Kentucky Fruit Filling (recipe below)

Directions:

1. Preheat oven to 350 degrees F (175 degrees C). Grease two 9 inch, round cake pans, and line with parchment paper.
2. Combine 2 1/2 cups flour, salt, and spices.
3. Dissolve soda in buttermilk: stir well.
4. Cream butter or margarine. Gradually add sugar, beating well.
5. Add eggs, one at a time, beating well after each addition.
6. Mix flour mixture into creamed mixture alternately with buttermilk mixture, beginning and ending with flour mixture. Dredge dates and pecans in remaining 1/2 cup flour, and fold into batter.
7. Carefully fold grape jam into batter. Pour batter into prepared pans.
8. Bake for 40 to 45 minutes, or until a wooden toothpick inserted in center comes out clean.
9. Cool in pans for 10 minutes.
10. Remove layers from pans, and cool completely.

11. Spread hot Kentucky Fruit Filling (recipe below) between the layers and on top of the cake.
12. Serve while listening to some Kentucky Bluegrass music and enjoy!

Kentucky Fruit Filling

To spread on the Kentucky Heritage Jam Cake.

Ingredients:

1 cup dates, pitted and chopped
1 cup chopped raisins 1 large orange
1/3 cup white sugar
1/4 cup orange juice

Directions:

1. Cut orange into sections, and remove the seeds. Grind the sections, peels and all.
2. Combine dates, raisins, and ground orange in a medium saucepan and stir well.
3. Stir in sugar and orange juice. Cook over medium heat, stirring constantly, until mixture is thickened.
4. Spread hot filling between layers or on top of cake.
5. Serve while listening to some Kentucky Bluegrass music and enjoy!

Kentucky Henry Bain's Sauce

Henry Bain (1863–1928) was one of the first employees and eventually a head waiter at the Pendennis Club, which was founded in 1881.
He is credited with creating his namesake sauce for steaks and the local game animals brought in by members for preparation.
A potent sauce for serving with game meat.

Ingredients:

1 (17 oz.) jar mango or peach chutney
4 1/2 oz. pickled walnuts (optional)
1 (14 oz.) bottle ketchup
1 (10 fl. oz.) bottle steak sauce
1 (10 fl. oz.) bottle Worcestershire sauce
1 (12 oz.) bottle tomato-based chili sauce
1 dash hot pepper sauce (such as Tabasco), or to taste

Directions:

1. Mix chutney, pickled walnuts, ketchup, steak sauce, Worcestershire sauce, chili sauce, and hot pepper sauce in a large bowl.
2. Refrigerate until ready to use. Serve at room temperature.
3. Serve while listening to some Kentucky Bluegrass music and enjoy!

Kentucky Derby Pie

Ingredients:

1 1/4 cups chopped pecans
4 large eggs
3/4 cup brown sugar
3/4 cup light corn syrup
1/2 cup all-purpose flour
1/2 cup butter, melted and cooled
1/4 cup white sugar
2 tbsps. bourbon
1 1/2 tsps. vanilla extract
3/4 cup miniature semisweet chocolate chips
1 (9 inch) unbaked deep dish pie crust

Directions:

1. Preheat oven to 300 degrees F (150 degrees C).
2. Spread pecans over a cookie sheet.
3. Bake pecans in preheated oven until toasted, about 1 hour, stirring every 15 minutes.
4. Check pecans after 30 minutes.
5. Allow pecans to cool completely.
6. Increase oven temperature to 350 degrees F (175 degrees C).
7. Whisk eggs, brown sugar, light corn syrup, flour, butter, white sugar, bourbon, and vanilla extract together in a bowl until smooth. Fold pecan pieces and chocolate chips into the egg mixture until combined; pour into prepared pie crust.
8. Bake in preheated oven until pie is set, 50 to 60 minutes.
9. Serve while listening to some Kentucky Bluegrass music and enjoy!

Louisville Benedictine Spread

Ingredients:

2 English cucumbers - peeled and cut into 2-inch chunks
2 tbsps. minced white onion
1 (8 oz.) package cream cheese, softened
1/2 tsp. dried dill
1 dash hot pepper sauce (such as Tabasco®)
1 drop green food coloring, or as needed
Cayenne pepper, or to taste

Directions:

1. Process cucumber chunks in a food processor until finely chopped.
2. Put chopped cucumber and white onion in a piece of cheesecloth and twist to squeeze into a bowl as much liquid as possible from the vegetables, reserving the liquid.
3. Assure the food processor bowl is dry before returning cucumber and onion mixture to the food processor.
4. Add cream cheese, dill, hot pepper sauce, green food coloring, and cayenne pepper.
5. Process the mixture until smooth, scraping down the sides of the food processor bowl a few times to make sure everything is integrated. If too thick, add reserved liquid a tsp. at a time.
6. Serve while listening to some Kentucky Bluegrass music and enjoy!

Kentucky Modjeska Candy

Ingredients:

2 cup sugar
2 tbsp. butter
1 1/4 cup white corn syrup
1 tsp. vanilla
2 cup heavy cream
Pinch of salt
3/4 lb. large marshmallows, cut in half with scissors

Directions:

1. Combine sugar, 1 cup of cream, butter, syrup, and salt in a heavy 3 or 4 quart saucepan.
2. Put remaining cream in a small pan and heat it separately.
3. Bring sugar-cream-butter mixture to boil, stirring constantly.
4. Wipe down sides of pan with wet cloth or cover with lid briefly to dissolve remaining sugar crystals.
5. When it begins a rolling boil, dribble the hot cup of cream into the boiling mixture, stirring. Don't let the boiling stop. Cook over medium heat, stirring as necessary to prevent scorching until thermometer registers 238 degrees. Remove from heat and stir in vanilla.
6. Allow cooked caramel to stand 10 minutes before starting to dip.
7. Drop marshmallow half into caramel, then with fork, turn it over to coat completely and lift out, pulling the fork over edge of pan so surplus runs back into pan.
8. Place each piece on buttered or oiled surface, such as cookie sheets or waxed paper.
9. When set, wrap each piece separately in waxed paper.
10. (You can also melt Kraft caramels or use the sheets of caramel for wrapping apples.)

11. Dip in melted caramels or cut sheets and wrap around marshmallow and place in oven as for apples.
12. Serve while listening to some Kentucky Bluegrass music and enjoy!

Kentucky Fried Chicken

Ingredients:

2 eggs, beaten
1 1/2 cups milk
1 cup flour
3/4 cup fine bread crumbs
1 tsp. Knorr chicken bouillon
1/2 tsp. salt
1/2 tsp. garlic powder
1/4 tsp. onion powder
1/2 tsp. paprika
1 pinch ground sage
1 tbsp. freshly chopped parsley
2 large cloves garlic, pressed
1/2 tsp. soy sauce
1 tsp. black pepper
1 tbsp. Instant (Wondra) flour
Additional flour for separate pre-coating
5-6 cups non-hydrogenated Crisco or peanut oil
1 frying chicken, cut in pieces

Directions:

1. Pour the oil into a deep pan suitable for frying, and then heat over medium heat to about 360 degrees F.
2. In a small bowl beat the egg, milk, and soy sauce, then stir in 1/2 tsp. Knorr chicken bouillon.
3. Put the garlic cloves through a garlic press and add to the egg mixture.
4. Add half of the parsley and 1 tbsp. Wondra flour and stir well.
5. In a separate bowl, combine the 1 cup flour and the bread crumbs, and the remaining ingredients.
6. Mix well with a fork.
7. Put about 1/2 cup additional flour in a separate small bowl.

8. Use this to dip each chicken piece, prior to dipping in the milk and seasonings.
9. Roll each piece of chicken around until well covered, first in plain flour, then in milk mixture, then in flour/bread crumbs mixture.
10. Gently place the chicken pieces into the hot oil and allow to become a golden color.
11. Drain on paper towels.
12. Serve while listening to some Kentucky Bluegrass music and enjoy!

Kentucky Style Scalloped Potatoes

Ingredients:

4-5 large potatoes
1/4 lb. butter (1 stick)
salt and pepper, to taste
1 Vidalia or sweet onion, thinly sliced
1 tbsp. fresh parsley, minced
1/4 tsp. paprika (optional)
2 tbsps. bread crumbs tossed in melted butter

Directions:

1. Peel and thinly slice raw potatoes. Butter a casserole or pyrex dish.
2. Spread the bottom evenly with a layer of potatoes, and season with salt, pepper, butter, a bit of onion chopped fine, if desired; sprinkle with a little flour.
3. Follow with another layer of potatoes, onion, and seasoning.
4. Continue layering potatoes until the dish is filled.
5. For extra color and flavor, potatoes may be sprinkled with parsley, bread crumbs tossed in melted butter, with a dusting of paprika on top.
6. Just before baking, pour a quart of hot milk over the potatoes.
7. Bake at 350 degrees F for 45 minutes.
8. Serve while listening to some Kentucky Bluegrass music and enjoy!

Kentucky Chicken with Bourbon Jelly

Ingredients:

4 chicken breasts
1 jar Kentucky bourbon jelly
1/2 cup chicken stock
Salt and pepper
1/2 cup dry white wine

Directions:

1. Sprinkle salt and pepper on both sides of the chicken breasts and cook them in the hot oil at medium heat.
2. Turn the breasts and continue cooking until done.
3. Take out the breasts and put them onto large plates and pour off the grease from the pan. Deglaze the pan with white wine and chicken stock.
4. Pour sauce over the breasts and spread all over with the Kentucky bourbon jelly.
5. Serve while listening to some Kentucky Bluegrass music and enjoy!

Kentucky Style Carrots

Ingredients:

3 lb. carrots
1/2 stick butter
1 tsp. cinnamon
1/4 cup brown sugar
1/4 cup orange marmalade

Directions:

1. Peel and cook carrots until tender.
2. Drain.
3. Melt butter over carrots and add other ingredients.
4. Add brown sugar and marmalade to carrots.
5. Serve while listening to some Kentucky Bluegrass music and enjoy!

Kentucky Style Chicken and Dumplings

Ingredients:

2 qts. chicken broth
2 cups all-purpose flour
1/2 tsp. salt
Shortening the size of an egg
1/2 cup water

Directions:

1. Combine flour and salt, add shortening.
2. Mix in well with 2 knives or a pastry mixer.
3. Add water 1/2 at a time, mix well.
4. Roll out on floured surface until thick, cut into small squares.
5. Drop into boiling broth.
6. Cook uncovered about 15 minutes.
7. Serve while listening to some Kentucky Bluegrass music and enjoy!

Kentucky Green Tomato Pickles

Ingredients:

1 gallon green tomatoes
6 onions
1/2 cup salt
1/2 cup vinegar
2 hot peppers
1 tbsp. ground mustard
1 tbsp. mustard seed
1 tbsp. celery seed
1 tbsp. allspice
1 tbsp. horseradish
1 tbsp. whole black pepper
4 cup vinegar

Directions:

1. Slice tomatoes and onions.
2. Sprinkle with salt and let stand overnight.
3. Boil vinegar, sugar with seasonings 5 minutes.
4. Tie spices in a piece of white cloth before cooking in vinegar.
5. Add tomatoes and onions.
6. Simmer for 30 minutes.
7. Pour into sterilized jars and seal at once.
8. Use cherry tomatoes or Italian tomatoes, cut in half.
9. Serve while listening to some Kentucky Bluegrass music and enjoy!

Kentucky Apple Dumplings

Ingredients:

2 cup apples, peeled, sliced thin
1 cup sugar
1 1/2 tsp. cinnamon
Dough enough for 2 pie shells

Directions:

1. Peel, slice and mix apples with sugar and cinnamon.
2. Roll out crust and cut in 4 inch squares.
3. Place apple mixture in the middle of each square. Pinch each square together.
4. To close the mix, use a little water on hands to seal well.
5. Place in a buttered pan and bake at 400 degrees until apples are done.
6. Serve with Orange Sauce. (recipe below)

Orange Sauce Ingredients:

1 cup orange juice
1 cup apple juice
1 1/2 cup sugar
2 tsp. cinnamon
1/4 cup butter
3 tbsp. cornstarch

Directions:

1. Mix cornstarch with sugar and some juice until smooth.
2. Add butter and remaining juice, cook until clear, stirring constantly.
3. Serve while listening to some Kentucky Bluegrass music and enjoy!

Kentucky Beer Cheese

Ingredients:

1 cup beer
1 lb. extra-sharp Cheddar cheese, shredded
2 cloves garlic, minced
1 tsp. dry mustard powder
1/2 tsp. freshly ground black pepper
1/2 tsp. cayenne pepper
1/4 tsp. salt
1/4 tsp. hot pepper sauce (such as Tabasco®)
1/4 tsp. Worcestershire sauce
1 pinch cayenne pepper, or to taste

Directions:

1. Pour beer into a bowl and whisk until beer loses its carbonation, about 30 seconds.
2. Set aside.
3. Place shredded cheese into the work bowl of a food processor.
4. Add garlic, dry mustard powder, black pepper, 1/2 tsp. cayenne pepper, salt, hot sauce, Worcestershire sauce, and flat beer.
5. Process until smooth and creamy, pulsing a few times, scraping the sides, and blending for about 2 total minutes.
6. Taste and adjust seasoning.
7. If adding more seasoning, pulse a few times to mix.
8. Transfer cheese spread to a bowl and sprinkle with a pinch of cayenne pepper.
9. Spread tastes best when refrigerated overnight to blend flavors, but it can be served right away if needed.

Kentucky Baked Beans

Ingredients:

6 strips of thick cut bacon
2 med. onions, chopped
1 red bell pepper, chopped
1 jalapeño, chopped
1 can (15 oz.) red kidney beans, drained and rinsed
1 can (15 oz.) white kidney beans, drained and rinsed
1 can (15 oz.) black beans, drained and rinsed
1/2 cup raisins
3/4 cup Kentucky style BBQ sauce
4 tbsp. molasses, any grade
1/4 cup Kentucky Bourbon
2 tsps. dry mustard
1/4 tsp. salt
1/4 tsp. black pepper
1 bay leaf

Directions:

1. Use a 2 quart or larger pot or Dutch oven.
2. Cook the bacon over a medium heat.
3. When it begins to brown, flip it, brown the other side, but remove it before it gets hard and you can still cut it without crumbling.
4. Pour off the bacon fat, leaving behind about 2 tbsps. and most of the brown bits dissolved in the fat.
5. Add the onions and peppers and cook them until they wilt.
6. Add the remaining ingredients.
7. Bring to a gentle boil over medium heat.
8. Turn it back to simmer for 30 minutes without a lid.
9. Stir and scrape the bottom with a wooden spoon every 10 minutes to prevent burning and sticking.
10. Try to keep the bay leaf submerged.
11. Remove the bay leaf.
12. Taste.

13. Add hot sauce if you like it spicier or add more molasses if you like it sweeter.
14. Add salt as needed.
15. Cook it longer if you want it thicker, or add water if you want it thinner.

Kentucky Baked Ham

Ingredients:

1 whole ham
1 can pineapple
1 cup brown sugar
1 can cherries

Directions:

1. Preheat oven to 350 degrees F.
2. Place ham in pan.
3. Slice the ham in middle, about 5 inches long.
4. Place brown sugar over ham.
5. Cover ham with pineapple using toothpicks.)
6. Put one cherry in the center of each pineapple ring with toothpicks.
7. Bake for 3 hours.
8. Serve while listening to some Kentucky Bluegrass music and enjoy!

Kentucky Bluegrass Salad

Ingredients:

1/2 cup vegetable oil
1/4 cup rice vinegar
1 tbsp. balsamic vinegar
2 tbsps. sugar
1 tsp. butter or margarine
3/4 cup walnuts
2 heads romaine lettuce, torn
2 pears, chopped
1 cup asparagus tips*
1/2 cup crumbled blue cheese
1/2 cup dried cranberries

Directions:

1. Whisk together first 4 ingredients.
2. Chill at least 1 hour.
3. Melt butter in a skillet over medium heat.
4. Add walnuts, and sauté 5 minutes or until lightly browned.
5. Remove walnuts with a slotted spoon.
6. Toss together lettuce, pears, asparagus, and toasted walnuts.
7. Sprinkle with cheese and cranberries; drizzle with dressing.
8. *1 cup broccoli florets or 1 cup snow peas may be substituted.
9. Serve while listening to some Kentucky Bluegrass music and enjoy!

Kentucky Bluegrass Fudge Pie

2/3 cup all purpose flour
1/2 cup unsweetened cocoa powder
1 1/2 cup chopped walnuts
1 cup sugar
2 eggs
3 tsp. vanilla
1/4 tsp. salt
1/2 cup butter
1 pt. ice cream (optional)

Directions:

1. Grease an 8 x 1 1/2 inch cake pan.
2. Preheat oven to 350 degrees F.
3. Combine flour, cocoa, and salt on wax paper.
4. Spread walnuts in a shallow pan. Toast in oven stirring often, for 10 minutes; cool; reserve.
5. Beat butter, sugar, eggs and vanilla in a medium size bowl until light and fluffy. Stir in flour mixture until well blended.
6. Stir in toasted walnuts.
7. Turn into prepared pan.
8. Bake for 30 minutes or until a wooden pick inserted in the center come out with moist crumbs.
9. Cool on wire rack.
10. Remove from pan.
11. Spoon ice cream onto center of pie.
12. Cut into pie shaped wedges.
13. Serve while listening to some Kentucky Bluegrass music and enjoy!

Kentucky Black Bottom Pie

Ingredients:

1/3 cup flour
1 cup sugar
1 stick butter
2 eggs, slightly beaten
1 (6 oz.) pkg. semi-sweet chocolate chips
1 cup chopped nuts
1 tbsp. vanilla flavoring

Directions:

1. Mix flour and sugar. Melt butter.
2. Mix sugar and beaten eggs.
3. Add to flour mixture. Add butter.
4. Add chocolate chips and vanilla.
5. Pour into unbaked pie shell.
6. Bake 50-60 minutes at 325 degrees or until done.
7. Serve while listening to some Kentucky Bluegrass music and enjoy!

Kentucky Bourbon Cake

Ingredients:

2 cups red candied cherries, about 1 lb. chopped
1 1/2 cup light seedless raisins
2 cups bourbon
1 1/2 cup butter
2 1/3 cups granulated sugar
2 1/3 cups dark brown sugar, firmly packed
6 eggs, separated
5 cups sifted cake flour
2 tsp. nutmeg
1 tsp. baking powder
4 cups shelled pecans (about 1 lb.)

Directions:

1. Combine cherries, raisins and bourbon.
2. Cover and let stand overnight at room temperature.
3. Drain the fruits and reserve the bourbon.
4. Cream butter with granulated and brown sugars until light and fluffy.
5. Beat in egg yolks, one at a time, beating well after each addition.
6. Combine 1/2 cup flour and the pecans, coating nuts well. Sift remaining 4 1/2 cups flour, nutmeg and baking powder together.
7. Add flour mixture and bourbon alternately to butter mixture, beating well after each addition.
8. Beat egg whites stiff and fold into batter.
9. Fold soaked fruits and pecans into batter.
10. Line greased 10" tube pan with waxed paper and grease paper.
11. Pour batter into pan. Bake in preheated 275 degree oven for 3 1/2 hours. Cool cake in pan and remove when cooled.
12. Fill center of cake with cheesecloth dipped in bourbon.
13. Wrap cake and cheesecloth in heavily waxed paper or aluminum foil.
14. Store in tightly covered container and keep in cool place.
15. Check cheesecloth occasionally for moisture.
16. If dry, saturate it with more bourbon. Makes 1 (10") cake that is better after maturing for several weeks.
17. Serve while listening to some Kentucky Bluegrass music and enjoy!

Kentucky Bourbon Apple Pie

Pie Ingredients:

1 cup all-purpose flour
1 tbsp. sugar
1/4 tsp. salt
1 (3 oz.) pkg. cream cheese, cubed
1/2 cup unsalted butter, cubed

Filling Ingredients:

6 cups peeled, thinly sliced cooking apples
1 cup plus 3 tbsp. sugar
3 eggs
3/4 cup butter, melted
1/2 cup chopped walnuts
2 tbsp. bourbon

Pie Directions:

1. In large bowl combine flour, sugar and salt.
2. With pastry blender cut in cream cheese and butter until mixture resembles coarse crumbs.
3. Knead into ball; flatten slightly. Cover and refrigerate one hour.
4. Roll out between 2 sheets waxed paper.
5. Peel off top paper; invert into 9 inch deep dish pie plate.
6. Flute edge.
7. Refrigerate one hour.

Filling Directions:

1. Arrange apples in pastry shell.
2. In medium bowl combine sugar, flour and eggs; stir with wire whisk until smooth.
3. Slowly stir in melted butter, then walnuts and bourbon.
4. Pour over apples. Bake 60 minutes at 375 degrees. Cool.
5. Before serving top with dusting of confectioners' sugar.
6. Serve while listening to some Kentucky Bluegrass music and enjoy!

Kentucky Chews

Ingredients:

50 light caramels (14 oz. pkg.)
1/3 cup evaporated milk
1 box German chocolate cake mix
3/4 cup melted butter
1/3 cup evaporated milk
1 cup chocolate chips

Directions:

1. Melt caramels and 1/3 cup evaporated milk over low heat. Stir, set aside.
2. Grease and flour 9x13 inch cake pan.
3. In large bowl, combine dry cake mix, butter, 1/3 cup evaporated milk and nuts.
4. Stir by hand until dough rolls together, press half of dough into pan.
5. Reserve the rest.
6. Bake 6 minutes at 350 degrees.
7. Sprinkle chocolate chips on hot crust, spread caramel mixture over chocolate chips.
8. Crumble reserved dough on top. Return to oven, bake 15-18 minutes.
9. Cool slightly. Refrigerate for 30 minutes to set caramel layer.
10. Serve while listening to some Kentucky Bluegrass music and enjoy!

Kentucky Breakfast Grits Cakes

Ingredients:

2 1/3 cups water
1 cup quick-cooking grits
5 tbsps. unsalted butter, divided
1 tsp. salt
1/8 tsp. ground black pepper
1/8 tsp. cayenne pepper (optional)
1/3 cup all-purpose flour
5 eggs, or more
Salt and pepper to taste
5 slices bacon, cooked and crumbled (or ham combined with the eggs when scrambling)
1/4 cup sliced grape tomatoes
3/4 cup shredded sharp cheddar cheese
2 tbsps. chopped scallions

Directions:

1. Bring 2 1/3 cups water to boil in a medium saucepan.
2. Stir in grits, reduce heat to low, and cook, stirring occasionally until grits reach porridge consistency, about 5 minutes.
3. Remove from heat and stir in 2 tbsps. butter, salt, black pepper and cayenne, if using.
4. Line a small rimmed baking sheet with plastic wrap.
5. Pour grits in the center and spread, using a spatula, to a thickness of 3/8 inch.
6. Let cool until grits are set, about 30 minutes.
7. Using a 3-inch cookie or biscuit cutter, cut out 12 circles from the cooled grits.
8. Dredge both sides of these grits cakes in flour.
9. Heat a large cast-iron pan over medium-high heat. Melt 2 tbsps. butter and swirl to coat the bottom.
10. Working with half the cakes at a time, cook until lightly browned, 1 1/2 to 2 minutes each side.

11. Carefully remove with a spatula and drain on a plate lined with a paper towel.
12. Add remaining 1 tbsp. butter to the pan and cook the remaining cakes.
13. Preheat broiler and line broiler pan with foil.
14. Scramble eggs in a small skillet.
15. Place cakes on the broiler pan. Spoon scrambled eggs onto cakes.
16. Top with bacon, tomatoes and cheese.
17. Broil until the cheese melts, 1 to 2 minutes.
18. Place grits cakes on a plate and sprinkle with the scallions.
19. Serve while listening to some Kentucky Bluegrass music and enjoy!

Kentucky Derby with Bourbon Whipped Cream

Ingredients:

1 cup all purpose flour
2 cups sugar
4 eggs
1 cup melted butter
4 tbsps. Maker's Mark bourbon
2 cups chopped walnuts
2 1/2 cups dark chocolate morsels
2 tsps. vanilla
2 pinches salt
Bourbon whipped cream (recipe follows)

Directions:

1. In the bowl of an electric mixer, mix flour and sugar.
2. Add eggs and butter, and mix on low to combine.
3. Add bourbon, walnuts, chocolate morsels, vanilla and salt.
4. Mix thoroughly on medium speed.
5. Pour into two 9-inch unbaked pie crusts and bake at 350 degrees for 45 minutes.
6. Let cool and serve with bourbon whipped cream.
7. Makes 2 pies.
8. Serve while listening to some Kentucky Bluegrass music and enjoy!

Kentucky Bourbon Whipped Cream

Ingredients:

1 pint whipping cream
2 tbsps. powdered sugar
1 tbsp. bourbon

Directions:

1. Chill a small bowl and beaters.
2. Pour cream, sugar and bourbon into bowl and beat with a hand-held electric mixer until stiff peaks form.
3. Store in refrigerator; it will stay stiff for a day or two.
4. Serve while listening to some Kentucky Bluegrass music and enjoy!

Kentucky Cabbage Casserole

Ingredients:

1 sm. head cabbage (1 lb.)
1 cup celery, sliced or chopped
1/4 tsp. salt
1 can cream of celery soup (undiluted)
1/3 cup milk
1 tbsp. minced onion
2 tbsp. butter
1/2 cup finely crushed butter crackers (Ritz or Townhouse)

Directions:

1. Knife shred cabbage to 4 cups.
2. Boil 5 minutes with celery and salt; drain. In 1 1/2-quart casserole, mix together soup, milk, onion, cabbage and celery.
3. Mix well.
4. Melt butter and mix crumbs in. Sprinkle over cabbage.
5. Bake at 350 degrees for 40 minutes.
6. Serve while listening to some Kentucky Bluegrass music and enjoy!

Bluegrass Beercheese Melts with Bourbon BBQ Glaze

Sandwich Ingredients:

12 slices bacon
1 stick butter, softened
1 tbsp. olive oil
2 small yellow onions, sliced thinly into rings
1 poblano pepper, julienne
1 green bell pepper, julienne
Bourbon BBQ Glaze:
1/2 cup ketchup
3 tbsps. barbecue sauce
3 tbsps. bourbon
2 tbsps. yellow mustard
2 tbsps. brown sugar

Beercheese Ingredients:

2 cups grated sharp Cheddar
1 tbsp. spicy steak sauce
1 clove garlic
1/4 tsp. garlic salt
1 tsp. cayenne pepper
1/4 cup plus 1 tbsp. flat beer
2 pounds freshly ground chuck
2 tsps. salt
2 tsps. freshly ground black pepper
Vegetable oil, for brushing grill
12 slices Texas Toast

Directions:

1. Preheat oven to 400 degrees F.
2. Lay out bacon strips on rimmed baking sheet pan, lined with parchment paper or foil.
3. Bake until brown and crisp, about 10 to 12 minutes, depending on thickness.

4. Remove, drain on paper towels, and set aside.
5. Alternately, bacon can also be cooked in the microwave or on the stovetop.
6. Preheat a gas grill, charcoal grill, or indoor grill to medium-high heat.
7. In a large skillet over medium-high heat, melt 1 tbsp. butter and 1 tbsp. olive oil.
8. Set aside remaining butter for bread. Saute onions and both peppers until soft and caramelized.
9. Meanwhile, combine ketchup, barbecue sauce, bourbon, mustard, and sugar in a small saucepan.
10. Bring to a light simmer and continue to cook until sugar is dissolved and sauce is thick, about 3 to 4 minutes.
11. For Beercheese, combine first 5 ingredients in food processor, and with machine running, drizzle in beer until mixture is smooth and well combined.
12. Divide ground chuck into 6 square-shaped patties, approximately the size of Texas toast.
13. Season with salt and pepper. Brush grill with vegetable oil.
14. Place patties on grill and cook, turning once until done, approximately 5 to 7 minutes until desired doneness.
15. Once flipped, brush tops of patties with BBQ glaze.
16. Meanwhile, lightly butter both sides of each slice of Texas toast and grill on either side for 1 to 2 minutes along outer edges of grill, until lightly browned and toasted.
17. Spread 6 slices of Texas toast liberally with beercheese.
18. Top with bacon strips and burger patties.
19. Top burgers with caramelized onion and pepper mixture.
20. Spread the remaining slices of toast with additional BBQ glaze, about 1 tbsp. per slice, and invert onto burger patties. Enjoy!
21. Serve while listening to some Kentucky Bluegrass music and enjoy!

Kentucky Chili

Ingredients:

1-1/2 lbs. ground beef
1 med. onion, chopped
2 cans (32 oz. each) tomato juice
1 cup water
1 can (16 oz.) chili beans, undrained
1 tbsp. chili powder
1 tsp. salt
1/2 tsp. pepper
8 oz. uncooked spaghetti, broken in half

Directions:

1. In a Dutch oven, cook beef and onion over medium heat until meat is no longer pink.
2. Drain.
3. Add the tomato juice, water, chili beans, chili powder, salt and pepper.
4. Bring to a boil.
5. Reduce heat.
6. Cover and simmer for 15-20 minutes.
7. Cook spaghetti according to package directions.
8. Drain and stir into chili.
9. Serve while listening to some Kentucky Bluegrass music and enjoy!

Kentucky Coleslaw

Ingredients:

3 cups shredded cabbage
1/2 cup shredded carrots
2 tbsp. sugar
4 tbsp. milk
1/4 cup buttermilk
1/4 cup sour cream, optional
Dash Tabasco sauce
1 tbsp. dry minced onion
1/4 tsp. celery seed
1/2 cup mayonnaise

Directions:

1. Marinate 3 cups shredded cabbage, 1/2 cup shredded carrots, 2 tbsps. sugar, 4 tbsps. milk in refrigerator overnight.
2. Drain well.
3. Mix cabbage with 1/2 cup mayonnaise, 1/4 cup buttermilk or sour cream, dash of Tabasco, 1 tbsp. dry minced onion and 1/4 tsp. celery seed.
4. Refrigerate 1 hour.
5. Serve while listening to some Kentucky Bluegrass music and enjoy!

Kentucky Pimento Cheese Sandwich

Pimento Cheese Ingredients:

8 oz. cream cheese, at room temperature
2 tbsps. mayonnaise
8 oz. sharp Cheddar, shredded
8 oz. aged Gouda, shredded
1 roasted red pepper, diced (about 1/2 cup)
Kosher salt and freshly ground black pepper

Sandwich Ingredients:

8 slices cracked wheat bread
3 tbsps. mayonnaise or softened
Unsalted butter

Cheese Directions:

1. Combine the cream cheese and mayonnaise in the bowl of a stand mixer fitted with a paddle attachment.
2. Mix on medium speed until smooth, about 1 minute.
3. Add the Cheddar and Gouda and mix to combine on low, about 1 minute.
4. Stir in the roasted red peppers by hand.
5. Taste and season with salt and pepper, but go heavy on the pepper; start with 1/2 tsp. and go from there.

Sandwich Directions:

1. On low heat, warm a cast-iron skillet.
2. Put a heaping 1/2 cup of the pimento cheese between 2 slices of bread.
3. Don't spread the mixture all the way to the crust because it will soften and spread as it heats in the skillet.
4. Repeat with the remaining bread and cheese.

5. Smear one side of each sandwich with mayonnaise, and place the sandwiches in the skillet mayonnaise-side down.
6. Smear the top pieces of bread with mayonnaise.
7. Cook until golden brown and the cheese has just started to melt, about 5 minutes.
8. Flip and cook the other side until golden, another 3 minutes.
9. Slice into halves or quarters and serve immediately.
10. Reserve any remaining pimento cheese in the refrigerator for up to 3 days.
11. Serve while listening to some Kentucky Bluegrass music and enjoy!

Bluegrass BBQ Chicken

Ingredients:

3/4 cup Worcestershire sauce
1/2 cup water
1/2 cup cider vinegar
1 tbsp. sugar
1 tsp chili powder
1/2 cup butter
1/2 (8oz) jar horseradish mustard
2 tsp salt
6 boneless chicken breasts

Directions:

1. Combine Worcestershire, water, vinegar, sugar, chili powder, butter, mustard and salt in a medium saucepan.
2. Bring to a boil, stirring occasionally.
3. Remove from heat and cool.
4. Place chicken in a ziplock bag.
5. Pour cooled marinade over chicken and refrigerate for 8 hours.
6. Remove chicken from marinade.

7. Grill chicken for about 8 minutes per side, or until done.

Kentucky Cornbread

Ingredients:

1 1/2 cup corn meal
3 tsp. baking powder
1 tsp. salt
1/2 cup oil
2 eggs
1 cup sour cream
1/4 cup water
1 cup (1 sm. can) cream style corn
1/2 lb. grated cheddar cheese

Directions:

1. Mix all ingredients except cheese.
2. Pour 1/2 batter into rectangular pyrex baking dish.
3. Sprinkle with cheese.
4. Add remaining batter.
5. Bake 30 minutes at 400 degrees.
6. Serve while listening to some Kentucky Bluegrass music and enjoy!

Kentucky Cream Candy

Ingredients:

3 cups sugar
1 cup cream
1/2 cup water
Pinch of soda

Directions:

1. Combine ingredients in a heavy greased saucepan.
2. Stir until boiling cook covered 3 minutes until sides of pan are washed free of crystals.
3. Uncover and cook, without stirring, to hard ball stage 262 degrees.
4. Remove from heat and pour onto a buttered marble slab or platter.
5. Let cool enough to handle easily.
6. Pull for about 15 minutes.
7. Cut into pieces with well buttered scissors.
8. Wrap candies in foil, store in a closed tin.
9. Serve while listening to some Kentucky Bluegrass music and enjoy!

Kentucky Eggnog

Ingredients:

6 eggs, separated
2 cups sugar
1/2 tsp. vanilla
2 cups bourbon
1 cup rum
1 cup milk
3 cups heavy cream
1 cup cognac

Directions:

1. Beat egg yolks until frothy.
2. Add sugar and vanilla and beat again.
3. Stir in bourbon, rum, milk, cream, and cognac.
4. Beat egg whites until stiff and fold into nog mixture.
5. Serve while listening to some Kentucky Bluegrass music and enjoy!

Kentucky Lace Cakes

Ingredients:

1 1/4 cups milk
1 tbsp. vinegar
1 egg
1 cup cornmeal
1/2 tsp. salt
1/2 tsp. baking soda
1 tbsp. butter, divided

Directions:

1. Combine the milk and vinegar in a bowl; set aside until the milk sours, about 5 minutes.
2. Stir the egg, cornmeal, salt, and baking soda into the milk mixture until evenly mixed.
3. Melt some of the butter in a large skillet over medium heat.
4. Pour 1/2 cup of the cornmeal mixture onto the skillet and cook until bubbles appear on the surface, 2 to 3 minutes.
5. Flip with a spatula and cook until browned on the other side, 1 to 2 minutes more.
6. Repeat until all batter is used.
7. Serve while listening to some Kentucky Bluegrass music and enjoy!

Old Fashioned Kentucky Nut Cake

Ingredients:

2/3 cup shortening
2/3 cup white sugar
3 eggs
2 2/3 cups all-purpose flour
1 tsp. salt
2 tsps. baking powder
1 cup milk 1 tsp. vanilla extract
1 1/3 cups chopped walnuts

Directions:

1. Preheat oven to 350 degrees F (175 degrees C).
2. Sift together flour, salt, and baking powder.
3. In a large bowl, cream shortening and sugar until fluffy. Beat in eggs one at a time.
4. Combine milk and vanilla, and add alternately with flour mixture to egg mixture. Fold in nuts.
5. Pour into a greased and floured 9 x 13 inch cake pan.
6. Bake for 35 to 40 minutes.
7. Cool on a wire rack.
8. Serve while listening to some Kentucky Bluegrass music and enjoy!

Kentucky Mint Julep

Ingredients:

10 mint leaves, plus a sprig for garnish
1 1/2 tsps. superfine sugar
Seltzer water
Crushed ice
2 1/2 oz. Kentucky bourbon whiskey

Directions:

1. Place the mint leaves in the bottom of an old-fashioned glass and top with the sugar.
2. Muddle these together until the leaves begin to break down.
3. Add a splash of seltzer water, fill the glass 3/4 full with crushed ice, and add the bourbon.
4. Top with another splash of seltzer, stir, and garnish with a sprig of mint.
5. Serve immediately.
6. Serve while listening to some Kentucky Bluegrass music and enjoy!

Kentucky Fried Apples

Ingredients:

3 med. tart cooking apples
1 cup sugar
1/3 cup butter

Directions:

1. Peel a 1 1/2" strip around the center of the apple.
2. This band will remove about a third of the apple peel.
3. Cut the apple in quarters. Next slice each quarter into 3 to 4 sections.
4. Place the apples, sugar and butter in a very heavy skillet or cooking pan. Cover and place on medium heat.
5. Allow 10 minutes or cooking time when mixture begins to cook.
6. Remove the cover and cook 5 to 10 minutes longer, until apples are tender and rather transparent.
7. You may need to reduce the heat to low during this final cooking stage.
8. Add a small amount of water if apples are too dry.
9. Add more sugar, depending on the tartness of the apples used to sweeten to taste.
10. Serve while listening to some Kentucky Bluegrass music and enjoy!

Kentucky Derby Cheese Grits

Ingredients:

4 cups boiling water
1 tsp. salt
1 cup instant grits
1 stick butter
1 roll garlic cheese
2 eggs
Milk

Directions:

1. Bring salted water to boil and slowly stir in grits.
2. Cook 3 minutes stirring constantly.
3. Remove from heat and stir in butter and garlic cheese.
4. Put eggs in cup and add milk to make 1 cup measure.
5. Beat well and add to grits mixture.
6. Bake in greased 2 quart casserole at 300 degrees F for 1 hour.
7. Serve while listening to some Kentucky Bluegrass music and enjoy!

Appalachian Fried Dandelions

Ingredients:

2 cups all-purpose flour
2 tbsps. seasoned salt
1 tbsp. ground black pepper
4 eggs
80 unopened dandelion blossoms, stems removed
1/2 cup butter

Directions:

1. Combine the flour, seasoned salt, and pepper in a mixing bowl until evenly combined; set aside.
2. Beat the eggs in a mixing bowl, then stir in the dandelion blossoms until completely coated.
3. Melt the butter in a large skillet over medium heat.
4. Remove half of the dandelions from the egg, and allow the excess egg to drip away.
5. Toss in the flour until completely coated, then remove from the flour, tossing between your hands to allow excess flour to fall away.
6. Cook the dandelions in the melted butter until golden brown, stirring occasionally, about 5 minutes.
7. Drain on a paper towel-lined plate.
8. Repeat with the remaining dandelions.
9. Serve while listening to some Kentucky Bluegrass music and enjoy!

Kentucky Fried Corn

Ingredients:

6 strips bacon, 1" cubes
4 ears corn, sweet or horse, scraped from cob
2 sm. cucumbers, thinly sliced
1 med. onion, minced or in rings
1 lg. egg
Salt, pepper & sugar to taste

Directions:

1. Lightly fry bacon, mix other ingredients thoroughly.
2. Pour into bacon grease.
3. Fry slowly so as not to brown too quickly, about 25 minutes.
4. Serve while listening to some Kentucky Bluegrass music and enjoy!

Appalachian Slaw

Ingredients:

4 cups chopped cabbage
1 tomato, chopped
1/2 cucumber, chopped
1/2 cup chopped onion
1 tbsp. sugar
1 tsp. salt
1/2 tsp. ground black pepper
1 tbsp. mayonnaise

Directions:

1. In a large bowl, stir together the cabbage, tomato, cucumber, onion, sugar, salt, pepper and mayonnaise.
2. Add additional mayonnaise to suit your taste.
3. Serve while listening to some Kentucky Bluegrass music and enjoy!

Kentucky Fried Steak

1 (2 lb.) steak
Salt and pepper
Flour
Water

Directions:

1. Beat steak with a meat hammer to flatten well.
2. Roll steak in flour, pepper and salt.
3. Fry until brown. Make gravy from the drippings.
4. Put steak in gravy and simmer a few minutes.
5. Serve while listening to some Kentucky Bluegrass music and enjoy!

Kentucky Peach Cobbler

Ingredients:

1 stick butter
1 cup self rising flour
1 cups sugar
1 cups milk
1 tsp. vanilla
1 can pie fruit (peaches, cherry, blueberry or apple)

Directions:

1. Melt butter in a 9 x 11 inch pan.
2. Mix flour, sugar and vanilla.
3. Add to melted butter.
4. Spread pie fruit on top.
5. Bake at 375 degrees for approximately 45 minutes until brown and bubbly.
6. Serve while listening to some Kentucky Bluegrass music and enjoy!

Kentucky Plum Cake

Wet Ingredients:

2 cups sugar
1 cup Crisco
1 tsp. red food color
3 eggs
2 sm. jars baby food plums

Dry Ingredients:

2 cups flour
1/2 tsp. soda
1/2 tsp. salt
1 tsp. cinnamon
1 tsp. cloves
1 cup nuts

Topping Ingredients:

3/4 stick butter
1 cup powdered sugar
2 1/2 tsp. lemon juice.

Cake Directions:

1. Beat together wet ingredients. Sift together dry ingredients.
2. Add flour mixture to wet ingredients, mix well.
3. Bake at 350 degrees for 1 hour in greased loaf pans.
4. Remove from pans when done and poke holes with fork throughout top.
5. Pour topping over cakes.

Topping Directions:

1. Heat to full boil 3/4 stick butter, 1 cup powdered sugar and 2 1/2 tsp. lemon juice.
2. Serve while listening to some Kentucky Bluegrass music and enjoy!

Kentucky Praline Popcorn

Ingredients:

4 qts. popped popcorn - salt lightly
2 cups coarsely chopped pecans
3/4 cup butter
3/4 cup brown sugar, packed

Directions:

1. In a large bowl, mix popcorn and pecans.
2. Combine butter and brown sugar in a small saucepan.
3. Heat, stirring popcorn mixture.
4. Mix well to coat popcorn evenly.
5. Serve while listening to some Kentucky Bluegrass music and enjoy!

Kentucky Egg Scramble

Ingredients:

6 slices lean bacon
1 tbsp. butter
1 cup fresh or frozen corn kernels
1/2 cup chopped green pepper
1/4 chopped pimento
6 eggs, slightly beaten
Salt and pepper to taste

Directions:

1. Cook bacon in heavy 10 inch skillet over medium heat until crisp; remove and drain on paper towel.
2. Reserve 3 tbsps. of bacon drippings in skillet.
3. Add butter and corn.
4. Cook and stir for 1 to 2 minutes. Stir in green pepper and pimento and continue cooking until vegetables are tender, about 3 minutes.
5. Season eggs with salt and pepper.
6. Pour beaten eggs in skillet.
7. As mixture begins to set at bottom and side, gently lift cooked portions with spatula so that thin, uncooked portion can flow to bottom.
8. Avoid constant stirring.
9. Cook until eggs are thickened through but still moist, 3 to 5 minutes. Makes 6 servings.
10. Serve while listening to some Kentucky Bluegrass music and enjoy!

Kentucky Spiced Tea

Ingredients:

1/4 cup tea leaves
4 cups cold water
1/3 cup fresh orange juice
1 tsp. nutmeg
1 tsp. cloves
2 cups sugar
2/3 cup fresh lemon juice
12 cups boiling water
1 tsp. cinnamon
1 tsp. allspice

Directions:

1. Put sugar, cold water, and spices (tied in a bag) in enamel or stainless steel boiler.
2. Bring to a boil and boil 10 minutes.
3. Put in tea leaves (tied in a bag).
4. Add 12 cups boiling water and juices.
5. Steep for 5 minutes. Strain if desired.
6. Add lemon slices and cinnamon sticks to each cup when serving.
7. Serve while listening to some Kentucky Bluegrass music and enjoy!

Kentucky Style Green Beans

Ingredients:

4 cups trimmed heirloom green beans
1 slice bacon
1 clove garlic, minced
1 tsp. olive oil, or as needed
1/2 tsp. sea salt
1 pinch coarsely
Ground black pepper to taste

Directions:

1. Pour about 1 inch of water into a saucepan.
2. Add green beans, bacon, garlic, olive oil, sea salt, and pepper.
3. Bring the water to a boil, reduce heat to medium, and place a cover on the saucepan.
4. Cook beans until tender, 7 to 10 minutes.
5. Serve while listening to some Kentucky Bluegrass music and enjoy!

Kentucky Shaker Corn Sticks

Ingredients:

1 1/2 cups cornmeal
1/2 cup white sugar
1 1/4 tsps. salt
1 cup boiling water
1 quart vegetable oil for frying

Directions:

1. Stir the cornmeal, sugar, salt, and water together in a mixing bowl until a dough has formed.
2. Set aside to cool for 10 minutes.
3. Once cool enough to handle, place a spoonful of dough into the palm of your hand.
4. Roll the into a sausage shape.
5. Repeat with the remaining dough and cheese.
6. Heat oil in a large skillet to 375 degrees F (190 degrees C).
7. Cook the corn sticks in the hot oil until they turn golden brown and float to the top of the oil, about 4 minutes per side.
8. Drain on a paper towel-lined plate before serving.

Kentucky Bourbon Burgers

Ingredients:

3/4 pound ground venison
1/4 pound ground beef
6 fl. oz. cherry-flavored Kentucky bourbon whiskey, or more as desired
5 slices bacon, cooked and crumbled
1 tsp. freshly cracked black pepper
1 cup barbeque sauce
4 slices pepper Jack cheese

Directions:

1. Preheat an outdoor grill for medium-high heat and lightly oil the grate.
2. Combine venison and ground beef together in a bowl.
3. Add bourbon; set aside until liquid is absorbed, about 10 minutes.
4. Add bacon and black pepper; mix until thoroughly combined.
5. Form into 4 equal-sized burger patties.
6. Cook burgers on preheated grill, basting with barbeque sauce throughout cooking, until no longer pink in the center and the juices run clear, about 5 minutes per side.
7. An instant-read thermometer inserted into the center should read at least 165 degrees F (74 degrees C).
8. Top burgers with pepper jack cheese and cook until cheese is melted, about 1 minute.
9. Serve while listening to some Kentucky Bluegrass music and enjoy!

Kentucky Derby Salsa

Ingredients:

4 ears corn on the cob with husks
2 (15 oz.) cans no-salt-added black beans, drained and rinsed
6 Roma (plum) tomatoes, chopped 1 green bell pepper, chopped
1 red onion, diced
2 jalapeno peppers, chopped
1 lime, juiced
2 tsps. chopped fresh cilantro
2 cloves garlic, minced
1 (12 fluid oz.) can tomato juice
1 (14 oz.) can tomato sauce
1 pinch kosher salt, or to taste
1 pinch ground black pepper, or to taste

Directions:

1. Preheat grill for medium heat and lightly oil the grate.
2. Place ears onto the heated grill.
3. Roast corn until husks show burn marks on all sides and corn kernels are cooked through, about 20 minutes.
4. Turn ears of corn often.
5. Let corn ears cool until they can be handled; pull back husks and cut the roasted kernels from the ears.
6. Place kernels into a large salad bowl.
7. Lightly toss corn with black beans, plum tomatoes, green bell pepper, red onion, jalapeno peppers, lime juice, cilantro, and garlic.
8. Pour tomato juice and tomato sauce over the salsa; toss again.
9. Season with kosher salt and black pepper.
10. Serve while listening to some Kentucky Bluegrass music and enjoy!

Kentucky Derby Chocolate Chip Cookies

Ingredients:

2 1/4 cups all-purpose flour
1 tsp. baking soda
1/2 tsp. salt 1 cup butter, softened
1/2 cup white sugar
1 cup packed brown sugar
2 eggs
5 tbsps. Kentucky bourbon
1 1/2 cups chopped pecans
1 1/2 cups semisweet chocolate chips

Directions:

1. Preheat the oven to 350 degrees F (175 degrees C).
2. In a medium bowl, stir together the flour, baking soda and salt with a fork.
3. Set aside.
4. Cream together the butter, white sugar, and brown sugar until smooth.
5. Beat in the eggs one at a time, then stir in the bourbon.
6. Stir in the flour mixture just until blended.
7. Fold in pecans and chocolate chips.
8. Drop by large spoonfuls onto ungreased baking sheets.
9. Bake in the preheated oven until the edges are lightly browned, about 10 minutes.
10. Cool on the cookie sheet for a minute, then remove to wire racks to cool completely.
11. Serve while listening to some Kentucky Bluegrass music and enjoy!

Kentucky Shaker Lemon Pie

Ingredients:

2 medium lemons
2 cups sugar
1 pastry for a 9-inch single-crust pie
4 eggs, beaten well
2 tbsps. all-purpose flour
1/4 tsp. salt

Directions:

1. Using a knife, trim each lemon to remove the stem end and tip.
2. Slice each lemon crosswise, as thinly as you can possibly do it, into paper-thin circles.
3. Scoop up as much of the escaping lemon juices as you work, and add them to the bowl of sliced lemons.
4. Chop the thinly sliced lemons coarsely, so that the largest pieces of lemon rind and pith are only 1 inch long, again gathering escaping juices back into the bowl for their flavor.
5. Add the sugar to the bowl of lemons, and stir to mix them together really well.
6. Cover and set aside at room temperature, for at least 3 hours and as long as overnight.
7. Stir occasionally with a big spoon, to mix everything together well.
8. Heat the oven to 450 degrees F. Line a 9-inch pie pan with crust, leaving a 1-inch overhang.
9. Add the eggs, flour, and salt to the bowl of sugary lemons. Stir to mix everything evenly and well.
10. Pour this filling into the piecrust.
11. Use a little water to wet the top rim of pastry around the piecrust. Roll the remaining dough into a 10-inch circle and place it carefully over the filling.
12. Trim away the extra pastry, leaving a 1-inch overhang extending beyond the rim of the pie pan.

13. Fold the crust up and over, and crimp it decoratively.
14. Or press the tines of a fork into the pastry rim, working around the pan to make a design.
15. Cut 8 steam vents in the top of the pie.
16. Place the pie on a baking sheet and place it on the middle shelf of the oven.
17. Bake for 15 minutes.
18. Reduce the heat to 375 degrees F and bake until the filling is bubbling and thickened, and the pastry crust is cooked and browned, 25 to 35 minutes more.
19. Place the pie on a cooling rack or a folded kitchen towel and let cool to room temperature.
20. Serve while listening to some Kentucky Bluegrass music and enjoy.

Kentucky Shaker Fried Chicken

Ingredients:

2 spring chickens, quartered
3 tbsps. soft butter
1 tbsps. fresh minced parsley
1 tsp. minced fresh marjoram (1/4 tsp. dried marjoram)
1/4 cup flour
salt and pepper
2 tbsps. butter
2 tbsps. lard
1 cup light cream

Directions:

1. Wash chickens well and quarter.
2. Rub thoroughly with soft butter and sprinkle generously with parsley and marjoram. Let stand at room temperature for one hour.
3. Roll in flour to which salt and pepper have been added. Heat heavy skillet, add butter and lard combined.
4. Cook chicken on all sides until golden brown.
5. Pour cream over it and let simmer, covered, for 20 minutes.
6. Serve while listening to some Kentucky Bluegrass music and enjoy!

Kentucky Shaker Tomato Pudding

Ingredients:

6 tbsps. butter
1 cup chopped onions
4 cups chopped skinned fresh tomatoes (4 cups canned diced tomatoes)
salt and pepper to taste
1/4 cup brown sugar
2 tbsps. chopped fresh basil
2 tbsps. chopped fresh parsley
1 1/2 cups small bread cubes
1 cup fresh buttered bread crumbs

Directions:

1. Melt 2 tbsps. butter in large saucepan and cook the onion until very tender.
2. Add tomatoes and stew them until they are reduced by half.
3. Add to them the salt, pepper, sugar, basil and parsley.
4. Pour the bread cubes into a 1 quart baking dish.
5. Melt remaining butter and pour it over bread.
6. Spoon the tomato mixture over all, sprinkle buttered bread crumbs on top.
7. Cover closely with aluminum foil or a lid. Bake 30 minutes at 350 degrees F.
8. Serve while listening to some Kentucky Bluegrass music and enjoy!

Kentucky Shaker Flank Steak

Ingredients:

3 pounds round beef, cut 1 1/2 inches thick
2 tbsps. flour
2 tbsps. butter
1 tsp. salt
1/4 tsp. pepper
1 stalk celery, chopped
1 carrot, chopped fine
1/2 green pepper, chopped fine
2 medium onions, chopped fine
juice 1/2 lemon
1/2 cup catsup

Directions:

1. Cut or score both sides of the meat diagonally and dust with flour.
2. Saute in heated butter until well browned on both sides.
3. Season with salt and pepper, then add all the chopped vegetables.
4. Add lemon juice and catsup.
5. Cover tightly and simmer very gently for 1-1 1/2 hours, or until the steak is tender when tested with a fork.
6. The vegetables cook down to a rich sauce to be served with the meat.
7. Serve while listening to some Kentucky Bluegrass music and enjoy!

Kentucky Shaker Spiced Apple Pudding

Ingredients:

3/4 cup butter
1 1/2 cups sugar
1 egg
1 1/2 cups sifted flour
1 1/2 tsps. baking soda
1 tsp. cinnamon
1/2 tsp. allspice
1/2 tsp. ground cloves
4 medium chopped apples, peeled, cored and chopped

Directions:

1. Cream butter and sugar in mixing bowl until light.
2. Beat in egg. Sift together all the dry ingredients.
3. Stir into creamed mixture. Stir in apples.
4. Turn into greased oblong pudding pan.
5. Bake in 375 degrees F. oven for 30 minutes.
6. Serve with heavy cream flavored with maple syrup or vanilla.
7. Serve while listening to some Kentucky Bluegrass music and enjoy!

Kentucky Spoonbread

Ingredients:

1/4 lb. butter
1 can of cream style corn
1 can of whole kernel corn
1 cup cultured sour cream
2 eggs, beaten
1 box of corn muffin mix

Directions:

1. Melt butter in a 8 x 12 inch pan or 9 x 13 inch pan.
2. Mix other ingredients all together in one bowl and pour in pan.
3. Take a spatula and mix around to mix in the butter throughout the ingredients and bake 1 hour for 350 degrees until center is firm.
4. Serve while listening to some Kentucky Bluegrass music and enjoy!

Kentucky Sausage Cheddar Spoonbread

Ingredients:

2 cups milk
1/2 cup yellow cornmeal
1/2 tsp baking powder
1 tsp salt
2 tbsp. melted butter
3 eggs, separated
3/4 cup shredded Cheddar
1/4 cup sliced scallions
1/3 lb. sausage, cooked and crumbled

Directions:

1. In a large pot, bring milk to a low simmer over medium heat.
2. Gently whisk in cornmeal and cook briefly, until mixture comes together.
3. Add baking powder, salt, and butter.
4. Whisk in the yolks and stir in the cheese, scallions, and sausage.
5. Beat egg whites until stiff and very gently fold into the cornmeal mixture.
6. Pour into individual buttered baking dishes or one large buttered baking dish.
7. Bake at 375 until spoonbread has risen and top is nicely browned, about 25 minutes for individual ramekins or 35-40 minutes for a large baking dish.
8. Serve while listening to some Kentucky Bluegrass music and enjoy!

Kentucky Style BBQ Pork Chops

Ingredients:

6 chops 1 - 1 1/4 inch thick
2 1/2 cups water
1 tbsp. sugar
3 black peppercorns
2 tbsp. butter
1/4 cup vinegar
3 tbsp. Worcestershire sauce
1/4 cup chopped onion
1 clove minced garlic
1 tsp. red pepper
2 tsp. chili powder
1 tsp. red pepper sauce
1 tsp. dry mustard

Directions:

1. Combine all but pork in a saucepan.
2. Bring to boil and simmer 5 minutes.
3. Best if sauce stands overnight. Warm sauce to serve.
4. Broil chops over low heat, 12 minutes per side.
5. Turn and brush with sauce frequently.
6. Serve while listening to some Kentucky Bluegrass music and enjoy!

Kentucky Pulled Pork

Ingredients:

6 or 7 lb. fresh pork shoulder
1 tsp. onion powder
1 tsp. garlic powder
1 tsp. sage
1 tsp. pepper
1/8 tsp. red pepper
1/2 tsp. MSG
4 tbsp. brown sugar
1/4 cup paprika

Directions:

1. Mix all the spices together and hand rub the shoulder on both sides.
2. Make sure you use all the mix. Pour the rest on top if left over.
3. Now set your oven to 400 degrees F.
4. Place shoulder in a roasting pan with 1 1/2-inch sides or more. Spray the pan with coating or grease with lard.
5. Place the shoulder in the pan, meat side up.
6. Place in oven; do not cover.
7. After 30 minutes, turn heat down to 250 degrees F.
8. Let bake for 6 hours. After pork comes out of the oven, take fork and punch in and pull.
9. Pork should be tender.
10. Pull enough for sandwich or have a meal and be sure to smother meat in barbecue sauce.
11. Serve while listening to some Kentucky Bluegrass music and enjoy!

Kentucky Mock Turtle Soup

Ingredients:

1 1/2 lbs. ground sirloin
6 stalks celery, chopped
2 cloves garlic, minced
1 cup chopped onion
3/4 cup butter
1 (15 oz.) can tomato puree
2 (14.5 oz.) cans chicken broth
2 (14.5 oz.) cans beef broth
1/2 cup flour mixed with 1 cup water
1/2 cup Worcestershire sauce
1 cup ketchup
1 tsp. hot sauce
2 bay leaves
1 1/2 tsp. thyme
Salt and pepper to taste
1 1/2 cups lemon juice
1/4 cup flat-leaf parsley, minced
6 hard-boiled eggs, chopped
6 slices lemon, for garnish
1 cup sherry, or to taste, optional

Directions:

1. On the stovetop, sauté the sirloin, celery, garlic, and onion in butter until meat is brown and veggies are translucent.
2. Add to the slow cooker.
3. Add tomato puree, chicken broth, beef broth, flour mixture, Worcestershire sauce, ketchup, hot sauce, bay leaves, thyme, salt, and pepper to the slow cooker.
4. Stir. Cook on low heat for 4 hours.
5. Add lemon juice, parsley, and eggs 30 minutes before serving.
6. Immediately before serving, remove bay leaves, add sherry to taste, and garnish with lemon slices.

Kentucky Brownies

Ingredients:

2 cup sugar
2 tbsp. vanilla
2 sticks butter, melted
1 1/2 cup self-rising flour
1/4 cup cocoa
3 eggs
1 tsp. salt
1/2 cup nuts

Directions:

1. Mix sugar and cocoa, stir in butter.
2. Add vanilla and eggs.
3. Mix well.
4. Add flour and salt.
5. Bake in ungreased oblong pan at 375 degrees for 30 minutes.
6. Serve while listening to some Kentucky Bluegrass music and enjoy!

Kentucky Eggs

Ingredients:

10 slices buttered bread, crusts removed
3 eggs, well beaten
1/2 lb. Longhorn cheese, grated
1 tbsp. Worcestershire sauce
2 cup milk
1/2 tsp. salt
1/2 tsp. prepared mustard

Directions:

1. Place slices of buttered bread in bottom of 9x13 inch pan.
2. Mix together beaten eggs, milk, Worcestershire sauce, salt, mustard and cheese.
3. Pour over bread. Set in broiler pan filled with 1/2 inch of hot water. Bake 30 minutes at 350 degree F.
4. Serve while listening to some Kentucky Bluegrass music and enjoy!

Kentucky Ham Biscuits

Ingredients:

2 cup flour
1 tsp. salt
2 tbsp. chopped parsley
2 tbsp. sugar
1/4 cup shortening
1 tbsp. baking powder
1 cup milk
1 (4 oz.) pkg. sliced cooked ham

Directions:

1. Preheat oven to 450 degrees. In large bowl with fork, mix flour, sugar, baking powder and salt.
2. Cut in shortening with pastry blender until mixture resembles coarse crumbs. Add milk, parsley, and ham; with fork, stir dough until just mixed.
3. Onto ungreased cookie sheet, drop by 1/4 cupfuls, 1" apart, to make 12 biscuits.
4. Bake 15 minutes or until golden.
5. Serve while listening to some Kentucky Bluegrass music and enjoy!

Kentucky Frogs' Legs

Ingredients:

24 frog's legs, skin removed
1 (4 oz.) packet saltine crackers, crushed
1 cup all-purpose flour
1/2 cup cornmeal
1 tsp. minced onion
2 tsps. salt
1 tbsp. ground black pepper
2 eggs
1/2 cup milk
2 cups vegetable oil for frying
1 cup peanut oil for frying

Directions:

1. Rinse the frog's legs and pat dry; set aside.
2. In a large resealable bag, combine the saltine cracker crumbs, flour, cornmeal, onion, salt and pepper.
3. Shake to mix. In a shallow bowl, whisk together eggs and milk.
4. Heat the vegetable oil and peanut oil in a large skillet over medium-high heat.
5. The oil should be about 1/2 inch deep.
6. Dip the frog's legs into the milk and egg, then dip into the cracker mixture until evenly coated.
7. Carefully place them in the hot oil.
8. Cook until golden brown on each side, about 5 minutes per side.
9. If the legs start to brown too quickly, reduce the heat to medium.
10. Drain on paper towels before serving.
11. Serve while listening to some Kentucky Bluegrass music and enjoy!

Kentucky Mountain Oysters (Lamb Fries)

If you have seen the movie Funny Farm, starring Chevy Chase, then you know what these are!

Ingredients:

12 lamb fries (testicles)
1 1/2 tsps. vegetable oil
3 Armenian chile peppers, seeded and sliced
1/2 onion, chopped
1/2 cup fresh spinach, trimmed and coarsely chopped
3 tbsps. butter
2 tbsps. lemon juice
1 1/2 tsps. lemon pepper
1/2 tsp. salt

Directions:

1. Slice each lamb fry in half lengthwise, and remove from the membrane.
2. Set aside.
3. Heat the vegetable oil in a large skillet over medium-high heat.
4. Stir in the lamb fries, and cook for about a minute until they begin to firm and change color.
5. Stir in the Armenian peppers, onion, spinach, and butter. Season with lemon juice, lemon pepper, and salt.
6. Cook and stir until the lamb fries are firm and white in the center, and the liquid from the vegetables has cooked down, 15 to 20 minutes.
7. Serve while listening to some Kentucky Bluegrass music and enjoy!

Appalachian Stack cake

Ingredients:

4 cups all-purpose flour
2 cups white sugar
1 tsp. salt
2 1/2 tsps. baking powder
4 eggs, beaten
2 tsps. vanilla extract
1/2 cup butter, melted
2 (6 oz.) packages dried mixed fruit
Ground cinnamon to taste
1/4 tsp. ground nutmeg
Salt to taste

Directions:

1. In a medium bowl, mix the flour, sugar, salt and baking powder.
2. Make a well in the center of the mixture and pour in the eggs, vanilla extract and butter.
3. Using the fingers, mix well, until a firm dough has formed.
4. Wrap in a clean tea towel and chill in the refrigerator 8 to 12 hours, or overnight.
5. Preheat oven to 400 degrees F (200 degrees C).
6. Turn a 9 inch round baking dish upside down, and lightly grease the surface.
7. Pinch off a portion of the dough and roll out into a 9 inch circle approximately 1/3 inch thick.
8. Continue this process with all the dough, making 5 to 7 layers.
9. Bake each layer individually in the preheated oven 8 minutes, or until lightly brown.
10. In a medium saucepan over medium heat, place the dried fruit in enough water to cover. Cook until soft and spreadable, but not runny, about 20 minutes.
11. Drain the fruit well.

12. Mix in the cinnamon, nutmeg and salt.
13. Stack the layers, spreading equal portions of the fruit mixture between each layer and on top of the final layer.
14. Chill in the refrigerator 8 to 12 hours, or overnight.
15. Serve while listening to some Kentucky Bluegrass music and enjoy!

Louisville Rolled Oyster

Ingredients:

½ cup all-purpose flour
1 tsp. baking powder
¼ tsp. salt
1 egg, well beaten
¼ cup milk (or more)
18 medium oysters, drained
1 cup white cornmeal
2 cups lard or 2 cups solid shortening

Directions:

1. Sift flour, baking powder and salt in a medium mixing bowl.
2. Beat together egg and milk; add to flour mixture and mix well.
3. Batter should be stiff, but if it is too stiff to coat the oysters, add additional milk.
4. Beat until smooth.
5. Put oysters in batter and stir to coat oysters well.
6. Scoop up three oysters at a time and form them by hand into a croquette.
7. Quickly roll croquette in cornmeal, covering it completely.
8. Repeat with remaining oysters.
9. After all croquettes have been formed, dip each again in batter and dust again with cornmeal.
10. At this point, oysters can be refrigerated until time to fry them.
11. Heat lard to 375 degrees F in a deep fryer.
12. Put 3 rolled oysters at a time in basket and lower into hot fat.
13. The rolled oysters should cook on all sides.
14. It may be necessary to turn them with a pancake turner.
15. Cook through, about 3 to 4 minutes total cooking time.
16. Drain on paper towels.

Kentucky Fried Catfish

Ingredients:

5 fresh catfish fillets
1 box of cornbread mix
1 medium egg
1/3 cup of milk
1/3 cup of pecans, finely crushed
2 tbsps. Creole seasoning
2 tbsps. olive oil for frying

Directions:

1. In a large bowl mix all the ingredients together except for the catfish.
2. Heat the oil in a large skillet over medium.
3. Dip the catfish fillets in the batter, coating both sides thoroughly, shake off excess batter and place in the hot oil.
4. Turning the fish often and adding more oil as needed for frying and sticking.
5. Fry the fish until is golden brown and tender.
6. Drain on paper towels.
7. Serve while listening to some Kentucky Bluegrass music and enjoy!

Kentucky Baked Catfish

Ingredients:

2 (7 to 8-oz.) catfish fillets
4 oz. butter
4 oz. dry white wine
1 tbsp. lemon juice
1 tsp. finely chopped garlic
1 tsp. chopped cilantro
Salt to taste
Pepper to taste
Paprika

Directions:

1. Season fish with salt and pepper.
2. Place fish in oval casserole dish.
3. Melt 4 oz. butter in small sauce pan.
4. Add wine and remaining ingredients, except the paprika.
5. Simmer about 2 minutes.
6. Remove from heat and spoon over fish.
7. Sprinkle paprika over fish.
8. Bake fish in 375 degree oven for 10 to 12 minutes, or until the fish is done.
9. Serve while listening to some Kentucky Bluegrass music and enjoy!

Kentucky Barbecued Catfish

Ingredients:

6 med. catfish
1 tsp. Worcestershire sauce
1/8 tsp. paprika
1/2 cup oil
1/4 cup white vinegar
1/4 cup catsup
4 tbsp. sugar
1/4 tsp. each salt & pepper

Directions:

1. Fillet and skin catfish; place in shallow dish.
2. Combine remaining ingredients in bowl; mix well.
3. Pour over catfish.
4. Marinate for 20 minutes.
5. Drain, reserving marinade.
6. Place catfish 4 inches above hot coals on greased grill.
7. Cook for 5 minutes on each side or until fish flakes easily, basting frequently with the reserved marinade.
8. Serve while listening to some Kentucky Bluegrass music and enjoy!

Kentucky Catfish Stew

Ingredients:

1/2 cup bacon drippings
2 lb. onions, chopped
2 cans condensed tomato soup
2 soup cans water
1 (8 oz.) bottle tomato catsup
1 tbsp. Worcestershire sauce
Few drops Tabasco
Salt and pepper to taste
4 lb. catfish, skinned and cleaned
4-6 lg. potatoes, pared and cubed

Directions:

1. Cook the onions in hot bacon drippings until they are soft.
2. Add tomato soup, water, catsup, Worcestershire, Tabasco, salt and pepper.
3. Blend well and bring to a boil.
4. Add catfish and potatoes.
5. Cover and cook over low heat for about 1 to 1 1/2 hours. Serves 8.
6. Serve while listening to some Kentucky Bluegrass music and enjoy!

Kentucky Fried Okra

Ingredients:

10 pods okra, sliced in 1/4 inch pieces
1 egg, beaten
1 cup cornmeal
1/4 tsp. salt
1/4 tsp. ground black pepper
1/2 cup vegetable oil

Directions:

1. In a small bowl, soak okra in egg for 5 to 10 minutes. In a medium bowl, combine cornmeal, salt, and pepper.
2. Heat oil in a large skillet over medium-high heat.
3. Dredge okra in the cornmeal mixture, coating evenly.
4. Carefully place okra in hot oil.
5. Stir continuously.
6. Reduce heat to medium when okra first starts to brown, and cook until golden, then drain on paper towels.
7. Serve while listening to some Kentucky Bluegrass music and enjoy!

Kentucky Okra and Tomatoes

Ingredients:

2 slices bacon
1 pound frozen okra, thawed and sliced
1 small onion, chopped
1/2 green bell pepper, chopped
2 celery sticks, chopped
1 (14.5 oz.) can stewed tomatoes
Salt and pepper to taste

Directions:

1. Place bacon in a large, deep skillet.
2. Cook over medium high heat until evenly brown.
3. Drain, crumble, and set aside.
4. Remove bacon from pan and saute okra, onion, pepper and celery until tender.
5. Add tomatoes, salt and pepper and cook until tomatoes are heated through.
6. Garnish with crumbled bacon, if desired
7. Serve while listening to some Kentucky Bluegrass music and enjoy!

Kentucky Pickled Okra

Ingredients:

1 1/2 pounds fresh okra
3 dried red chile peppers
3 tsps. dried dill
2 cups water
1 cup vinegar
2 tbsps. salt

Directions:

1. Divide the fresh okra evenly between 3 sterile (1 pint) jars.
2. Place one dried chile, and one tsp. of dill into each jar.
3. In a small saucepan, combine the water, vinegar and salt.
4. Bring to a rolling boil.
5. Pour over the ingredients in the jars, and seal in a hot water bath for 10 minutes.
6. Serve while listening to some Kentucky Bluegrass music and enjoy!

Kentucky Country Chicken Fried Steak

Ingredients:

4 (1/2 lb.) beef cube steaks
2 cups all-purpose flour
2 tsps. baking powder
1 tsp. baking soda
1 tsp. black pepper
3/4 tsp. salt
1 1/2 cups buttermilk
1 egg 1 tbsp. hot pepper sauce (e.g. Tabasco)
2 cloves garlic, minced
3 cups vegetable shortening for deep frying
1/4 cup all-purpose flour
4 cups milk kosher
Salt and ground black pepper to taste

Directions:

1. Pound the steaks to about 1/4-inch thickness.
2. Place 2 cups of flour in a shallow bowl.
3. Stir together the baking powder, baking soda, pepper, and salt in a separate shallow bowl; stir in the buttermilk, egg, Tabasco Sauce, and garlic.
4. Dredge each steak first in the flour, then in the batter, and again in the flour.
5. Pat the flour onto the surface of each steak so they are completely coated with dry flour.
6. Heat the shortening in a deep cast-iron skillet to 325 degrees F (165 degrees C).
7. Fry the steaks until evenly golden brown, 3 to 5 minutes per side.
8. Place fried steaks on a plate with paper towels to drain.
9. Drain the fat from the skillet, reserving 1/4 cup of the liquid and as much of the solid remnants as possible.
10. Return the skillet to medium-low heat with the reserved oil.

11. Whisk the remaining flour into the oil.
12. Scrape the bottom of the pan with a spatula to release solids into the gravy.
13. Stir in the milk, raise the heat to medium, and bring the gravy to a simmer, cook until thick, 6 to 7 minutes.
14. Season with kosher salt and pepper.
15. Spoon the gravy over the steaks.
16. Serve while listening to some Kentucky Bluegrass music and enjoy!

Kentucky Corn Pudding

Ingredients:

5 eggs
1/3 cup butter, melted
1/4 cup white sugar
1/2 cup milk
4 tbsps. cornstarch
1 (15.25 oz.) can whole kernel corn
2 (14.75 oz.) cans cream-style corn

Directions:

1. Preheat oven to 400 degrees F (200 degrees C).
2. Grease a 2 quart casserole dish.
3. In a large bowl, lightly beat eggs.
4. Add melted butter, sugar, and milk.
5. Whisk in cornstarch.
6. Stir in corn and creamed corn.
7. Blend well.
8. Pour mixture into prepared casserole dish.
9. Bake for 1 hour.
10. Serve while listening to some Kentucky Bluegrass music and enjoy!

Kentucky Whiskey Chicken

Ingredients:

2 pounds chicken thighs
Salt and ground black pepper to taste
1 1/4 cups pineapple juice
3 tbsps. bourbon whiskey, or more to taste
2 tbsps. soy sauce
3 cloves garlic
1 tbsp. brown sugar
1/4 tsp. ground black pepper
2 tsps. butter, or to taste
2 large mushrooms, sliced.
Add all ingredients to list

Directions:

1. Preheat an outdoor grill for high heat and lightly oil the grate.
2. Season chicken thighs with salt and pepper.
3. Cook the chicken thighs until no longer pink in the center and somewhat charred on the outside, about 7 minutes per side.
4. Let chicken cool until able to handle easily, cut into strips, and put into a large glass bowl.
5. Stir pineapple juice, bourbon whiskey, soy sauce, garlic cloves, brown sugar, and black pepper together in a saucepan over medium-low heat; stir until the sugar dissolves, bring to a simmer, and cook until thickened, 15 to 20 minutes.
6. While the sauce simmers, melt the butter in a small skillet over medium-high heat.
7. Saute mushrooms in hot butter until softened, 3 to 5 minutes.
8. Stir into the simmering sauce.
9. Pour the mushrooms and sauce over the chicken strips and toss to coat.

Kentucky Black Barbecue Sauce and Mutton Dip

Ingredients:

2 tsps. vegetable oil
1/4 cup minced onion
1/4 cup distilled white vinegar, plus
2 tbsps. distilled white vinegar
1/2 cup Worcestershire sauce, plus
2 tbsps. Worcestershire sauce
2 tbsps. light brown sugar, plus
1 tsp. light brown sugar
2 tsps. lemon juice
1/4 tsp. ground black pepper
1/4 tsp. Tabasco sauce
1/4 tsp. ground nutmeg
1/2 tsp. coarse salt

Directions:

1. Heat the vegetable oil over moderate heat.
2. Add the onion and cook for 5 minutes, or until the onion is soft and light golden brown.
3. Add the remaining ingredients, and simmer, uncovered, for 15 minutes.
4. The sauce will thicken slightly.
5. Serve while listening to some Kentucky Bluegrass music and enjoy!

Kentucky Country Style Quiche

Ingredients:

2 uncooked pie shells
1 1/2 pounds Swiss or Gruyere cheese (shredded or grated)
6 whole fresh eggs
1/2 cup heavy cream
1/2 cup milk
Dash of nutmeg
1 1/2 pounds fresh green beans
1/4 pound diced onion
10 oz. country ham (cooked or raw), diced

Directions:

1. Mix green beans, onion and country ham in pot with 6 cups water.
2. Simmer 2-3 hours, drain and cool.
3. Puree or chop to your desired size.
4. Divide bean and ham mixture evenly between pie shells.
5. Mix eggs, cream, milk, nutmeg, cheese and pepper.
6. Add salt to taste.
7. Pour over bean mixture in pie shells, lightly mix together.
8. Place on cookie tray in oven at 325 degrees for 20-30 minutes.
9. Quiche is done when wooden toothpick comes out clean.
10. Cut into wedges.
11. Serve while listening to some Kentucky Bluegrass music and enjoy!

Kentucky Hot Brown Pizza

Sauce Ingredients:

1 tbsp. unsalted butter
1 tbsp. all-purpose flour
1 cup whole milk
1/8 tsp. salt
1/8 tsp. freshly ground black pepper
1/8 tsp. freshly grated nutmeg
1 tbsp. sour cream
1 tbsp. grated Parmigiano Reggiano cheese

Pizza Ingredients:

24 oz. fresh pizza dough
1 cup shredded mozzarella
1/2 cup shredded Asiago cheese
1 1/2 cups chopped roasted turkey breast
1/2 cup chopped cooked bacon
1 cup chopped Roma tomatoes
1/4 cup chopped parsley

Directions:

1. To prepare sauce, melt butter in a medium saucepan over medium-low heat.
2. Whisk in flour until combined.
3. Cook about 2 minutes.
4. Whisk in milk, salt, pepper and nutmeg.
5. Add sour cream.
6. Bring mixture to a slow simmer.
7. The mixture will begin to thicken. Remove from heat.
8. Add cheese and stir until smooth.
9. To make pizza, preheat oven to 425 degrees F.
10. Roll pizza dough into a 14-inch round or square.
11. Place on baking sheet or pizza stone.
12. Spread sauce on dough and top with remaining ingredients in the order listed.
13. Bake 7 to 11 minutes, until puffy and golden brown.

Kentucky Chipotle Pork Quesadillas

Ingredients:

1 cup and 2 tbs. Evan Williams Bourbon
5 lbs pork loin roast
1/2 cup liquid smoke
1/2 cup brown sugar
1 tbs. salt
1/2 cup honey chipotle barbeque sauce
1 cup Monterey jack cheese
1 cup mayonnaise
1/2 packet powdered ranch dressing seasoning
1/3 cup pureed chipotles in adobe sauce
8 flour tortillas
Butter
Sliced red onion
Jalapenos

Directions:

1. Put pork roast, 1 cup bourbon, brown sugar, liquid smoke and salt into slow cooker.
2. If roast not covered with liquid, add enough water to cover meat.
3. Cook on low heat for 6-8 hours.
4. While pork is cooking make sauce: combine mayonnaise, pureed chipotles, ranch dressing seasoning and 1 tbs. bourbon and mix well.
5. Remove pork from cooker when done.
6. Add in barbeque sauce and 1 tbs. bourbon.
7. Shred pork and mix in sauce by pulling fork through meat.
8. Heat skillet to medium-high heat and add in some butter.
9. Assemble quesadillas by placing pork mixture and desired amount of cheese into one half of tortilla.

10. Fold over and place in skillet. Cook on both sides until slightly browned.
11. Remove from skillet and cut into wedges.
12. Serve with sauce and garnish with jalapenos and onion.
13. Serve while listening to some Kentucky Bluegrass music and enjoy!

Kentucky Butternut Squash Soup

Ingredients:

2 tbsp. butter
1 onion, diced
1 butternut squash, peeled, seeded, and cut into chunks
4 cups chicken stock, plus more if needed to thin
1 tsp cumin
Cayenne, optional
Salt and pepper, to taste

Directions:

1. In a large pot, melt the butter over medium heat.
2. Saute the onion until soft, then add the butternut squash.
3. Cover the vegetables with chicken stock and simmer until tender, about 20 minutes.
4. Using an immersion blender, puree the soup until smooth.
5. Add more chicken stock if a thinner soup is desired.
6. Season soup with salt, pepper, cumin and cayenne pepper.
7. Serve while listening to some Kentucky Bluegrass music and enjoy!

Kentucky Corn Chowder

Ingredients:

4 strips bacon, diced
2 ribs celery, diced
1 onion, diced
1/4 cup flour
4 cups chicken broth
2 cups whole milk
6 ears fresh corn
1 pound red potatoes, diced
Salt and pepper, to taste
Chopped parsley, to garnish

Directions:

1. Cook the diced bacon in a large soup pot until well browned.
2. Remove bacon with a slotted spoon and set aside.
3. Add the diced celery and onion to the bacon fat and saute until soft and lightly caramelized.
4. Add in the flour and cook, stirring well.
5. Add the chicken broth, milk, and potatoes and bring to a simmer, cooking until potatoes are tender.
6. Cut the kernels off the cob and add to the soup, along with any of the cob scrapings/corn milk that you can get by running the back of a knife down the cob.
7. Simmer until the corn is soft, but still crisp.
8. Season with salt and pepper, then garnish
9. Serve while listening to some Kentucky Bluegrass music and enjoy!

Kentucky Kale and Potato Soup

Ingredients:

4 tsps. olive oil
1 chopped yellow onion
3 cloves garlic, minced
1 box (48 oz.) low-sodium chicken broth
6 red potatoes, diced
1/2 cup chopped carrot
4 cups shredded kale
1/2 pound cooked chicken breast, shredded
1/4 tsp. black pepper

Directions:

1. In a large saucepan, heat the olive oil over medium heat for 1 minute.
2. Add chopped onion and garlic and cook uncovered for 5 minutes.
3. Add chicken broth, potatoes and carrot; cover and bring to a boil.
4. Reduce heat and simmer for 20 minutes.
5. Mix in the kale, chicken and black pepper.
6. Cover and simmer for 15 minutes or until kale is tender.
7. Serve while listening to some Kentucky Bluegrass music and enjoy!

Kentucky Onion Soup

Ingredients:

1 cup bread cubes
2 cups onions, thinly sliced
2 tbsps. oil
4 cups beef broth or stock
1 tbsp. butter, melted
2 tbsps. Parmesan or blue cheese, grated

Directions:

1. Toast bread cubes in a 325 degree oven until they are completely dried out and lightly browned.
2. Brown onions slightly in oil.
3. Bring stock to a boil, reduce heat.
4. Add onions and simmer, covered until onions are tender, about 15 minutes.
5. Toss toasted bread crumbs with butter and cheese and sprinkle on top of soup just before serving.
6. Serve while listening to some Kentucky Bluegrass music and enjoy!

Kentucky Bourbon Beef Stew

Ingredients:

2 lbs. chuck, cut into small pieces
Salt and pepper, to taste
1 tsp vegetable oil
1 large or 2 small onions, diced
3 cloves garlic, smashed
2 tbsp. tomato paste
4 cups beef stock, divided
1/2 cup bourbon
1 sprig rosemary
1 lb. carrots
1 lb. new potatoes, quartered
1 cup peas

Directions:

1. Season chuck pieces well with salt and pepper.
2. Heat the oil in a Dutch oven or large pot over high heat and brown 1/3 of the meat, allowing it to get a nice, dark sear on all sides.
3. Transfer it to a separate plate and continue to brown the meat in batches.
4. Once all the meat has been browned, add it all back to the pot and add the onions, garlic, tomato paste, 2 cups of the beef stock (or enough to cover the meat), bourbon, and rosemary.
5. Bring to a simmer and cook, partially covered, until beef is almost tender, about 1 to 1 1/2 hours.
6. Add the remaining beef stock and the carrots and potatoes and continue to simmer until vegetables are soft and potatoes begin to fall apart, about another 45 minutes.
7. At this point, the beef should be very tender.
8. If it is not, continue to simmer until it is.
9. add the peas to warm.
10. season well with bourbon salt and pepper.

Kentucky Mock Mint Julep

Ingredients:

4 mint sprigs
2 cups cold water
1 1/2 quarts Ale-8-One (6 pack of Ale-8-One)
1 1/2 cups sugar
3/4 cups fresh lemon juice
Thin lemon slices

Directions:

1. Rinse mint and discard stems.
2. Place sugar, water and lemon juice in medium sized bowl. Mix and stir in mint leaves.
3. Allow to stand for 30 minutes.
4. Fill a large pitcher with ice and stir liquid over ice.
5. Add Ale-8-One and lemon slices.
6. Pour into tall glasses.
7. Serve while listening to some Kentucky Bluegrass music and enjoy!

Kentucky Country Ham Balls

Ingredients:

2 pounds Kentucky country ham, ground
1 pound Parnell's Old Folks country sausage
2 cups dry bread crumbs
2 eggs
1 1/2 - 2 cups milk
2 cups packed brown sugar
1 cup water
1 cup white vinegar
1 tbsp. prepared mustard

Directions:

1. Combine ham, sausage, bread crumbs, and eggs in a large bowl, and mix well.
2. Add milk gradually (enough to moisten), and mix well. Shape into small balls, and place in a single layer in a baking dish.
3. Combine brown sugar, water, vinegar, and mustard in saucepan, and mix well.
4. Bring to a boil, then pour over ham balls.
5. Bake at 350 degrees for 45 minutes, basting after 25 minutes.
6. Serve while listening to some Kentucky Bluegrass music and enjoy!

Kentucky Bourbon Banana Bread

Ingredients:

3/4 cup chopped pecans
2 tbsps. bourbon
1/3 cup butter, softened
2/3 cup sugar
3/4 cup mini chocolate chips
1 cup mashed ripe bananas (about 3-4)
1/4 tsp. baking soda
1 3/4 cups all-purpose flour
2 tsps. baking powder
1/2 tsp. salt
2 eggs, well beaten
1/2 tsp. lemon juice

Directions:

1. Preheat oven to 350 degrees F. Coat a loaf pan with nonstick cooking spray.
2. In a medium-sized bowl, stir together flour, baking soda, baking powder and salt.
3. In another medium-sized bowl, mash bananas.
4. In a large bowl, cream butter with an electric mixer. Add well-beaten eggs, sugar and bananas.
5. Beat on medium speed for three minutes. Add lemon juice and bourbon, beat 30 seconds.
6. Add flour mixture and beat until just combined.
7. Fold in chocolate chips and chopped pecans.
8. Pour into pan and bake for 50 minutes to an hour or until a toothpick inserted in top center comes out clean.
9. Loaf should spring back slightly to the touch.
10. Cool completely on wire rack, wrap in foil.
11. Let sit 24 hours before eating.
12. Serve while listening to some Kentucky Bluegrass music and enjoy!

Kentucky Bourbon Pecan Sticky Buns

Ingredients:

2 eggs, beaten
2 tsps. sugar
1/2 cup softened salted butter
3/4 cup warm water
1 tbsp. active dry yeast
1/2 cup flour
1/4 cup whole-fat yogurt
1/2 cup whole-fat sour cream
1/2 cup sugar
2 tsps. salt
2 tsps. vanilla
1 tsp. dough emulsion (optional)
5 cup flour divided
1/2 cup buttermilk
1 1/2 cup heavy cream
1/4 cup light corn syrup
2 tsp. baking soda
2 tsp. vanilla
1/2 tsp. buttery dough emulsion (optional)
2 cup salted butter
1/4 cup bourbon
3/4 cup salted butter, soft
1/4 cup cinnamon
2/3 cup sugar
2 cups pecans

Dough Directions:

1. Combine the water, 2 t sugar, yeast, and 1/2 c flour in a medium non-metal bowl.
2. Stir a few times and set aside until doubled in size.
3. Meanwhile, combine the other dough ingredients (everything but the remaining flour) in a large, non-metal bowl or container.

4. Add the sponge once it has doubled in size, stir to combine, then stir in 4.5 cups of flour.
5. Stir together as well as you can in the bowl, then turn out onto the counter with the remaining 1/2 c flour.
6. Knead the dough until it is cohesive, soft and smooth.
7. Set aside in a greased, loosely covered container to rise.
8. Once it has gotten large and puffy, gently turn out on to the counter and halve.
9. Cover half with a damp towel or saran wrap.
10. Roll each half to around 10x15, keeping them as rectangular as possible.
11. Fill, roll gently towards yourself, cut evenly and set into prepared pans.
12. Allow them to rise again- another 45-60 minutes- until large and puffy.
13. Bake at 350 about 30-35 minutes, until golden brown.
14. Cool in pans for five minutes, then turn out onto parchment paper or silicone baking sheet.

Sauce Directions:

1. Combine the buttermilk, cream, corn syrup, baking soda, vanilla, and dough emulsion on a large saucepan.
2. The mixture will expand quite a bit so you want lots of headroom in the pot.
3. Cook over medium heat, stirring occasionally, until the mix feels hot.
4. Add the butter (bubbles!) and bring to a boil.
5. Reduce heat and simmer, stirring occasionally, until the sauce is the color of dark brown sugar, about 15-20 minutes.
6. Remove from the heat and stir in the bourbon carefully- it will bubble and spit.
7. Divide between two metal 13x9 pans.

Cinnamon Butter Directions:

1. Combine the butter, cinnamon, ad sugar in a medium bowl, stirring until well combined.
2. Toast the pecans over medium heat, stirring frequently, until they are golden brown and fragrant. Chop to a medium dice and set aside.
3. When filling your rolls, spread each half with half of the cinnamon butter mixture and top that with 1/2 the pecans.
4. Serve while listening to some Kentucky Bluegrass music and enjoy!

About the Author

Laura Sommers is **The Recipe Lady!**

She lives on a small farm in Baltimore County, Maryland and has a passion for food. She has taken cooking classes in Memphis, New Orleans and Washington DC. She has been a taste tester for a large spice company in Baltimore and written food reviews for several local papers. She loves writing cookbooks with the most delicious recipes to share her knowledge and love of cooking with the world.

Follow her on Pinterest:

http://pinterest.com/therecipelady1

Visit the Recipe Lady's blog for even more great recipes:

http://the-recipe-lady.blogspot.com/

Visit her Amazon Author Page to see her latest books:

amazon.com/author/laurasommers

Follow the Recipe Lady on Facebook:

https://www.facebook.com/therecipegirl

Follow her on Twitter:

https://twitter.com/TheRecipeLady1

Other Books by Laura Sommers

- Recipes for Chicken Wings
- 50 Super Awesome Salsa Recipes!
- Delicious Chip Dip Cookbook
- Authentic Traditional Memphis, Tennessee Recipes

Made in United States
North Haven, CT
06 May 2023